ONE JUMP AHEAD

Prince Hal at Lucerne after winning the Prix du Pilate

PAT SMYTHE

ONE JUMP
AHEAD

CASSELL & CO LTD
LONDON

CASSELL & CO LTD
37–38 St. Andrew's Hill, Queen Victoria Street
London, E.C.4

and at

31/34 George IV Bridge, Edinburgh
210 Queen Street, Melbourne
26/30 Clarence Street, Sydney
24 Wyndham Street, Auckland, New Zealand
1068 Broadview Avenue, Toronto 6
P.O. Box 275, Cape Town
P.O. Box 11190, Johannesburg
P.O. Box 189, Bridgetown, Barbados
Munsoor Building, Main Street, Colombo 11
Haroon Chambers, South Napier Road, Karachi
13/14 Ajmeri Gate Extension, New Delhi 1
15 Graham Road, Ballard Estate, Bombay 1
17 Chittaranjan Avenue, Calcutta 13
Macdonald House, Orchard Road, Singapore 9
P.O. Box 959, Accra, Gold Coast
Avenida 9 de Julho 1138, São Paulo
Galeria Güemes, Escritorio 554/59 Florida 165, Buenos Aires
Marne 5b, Mexico 5, D.F.
25 rue Henri Barbusse, Paris 5e
25 Ny Strandvej, Espergaerde, Denmark
Kauwlaan 17, The Hague

Set in 12 *on* 13 *point Bembo type and
printed in Great Britain by Wyman & Sons Ltd., London, Reading and Fakenham*
F.756

This book is dedicated
to the horses that give
us all so much pleasure

CONTENTS

ILLUSTRATIONS

[ix]

ILLUSTRATIONS

following page

[x]

ILLUSTRATIONS

[xi]

CHAPTER I

At Home

WHEN mother and father were married, they called their first little house in East Sheen 'Quien Sabe', for 'who knows' what life may bring in its train? I was born there, and little did I think when playing in the comparative freedom of Richmond Park and on Barnes Common that, by the time I was ten, we would have moved from town to the country.

This move was necessary as my father could no longer work through becoming slowly crippled by rheumatoid arthritis. Mother found us a house on the edge of the Cotswolds with a wonderful view over the Gloucester vale to the Welsh mountains beyond. Nothing could really compensate for my father's illness, but I was in my element with the smallholding of animals that we slowly gathered around us.

We had brought my pony Pixie with us from London, and had accumulated one or two other ponies, as well as some polo ponies. These belonged to my uncle, Lieutenant-Colonel Gordon Smythe, who lived at Swindon Village the other side of Cheltenham. We had often been there for Christmas holidays and loved the old Manor House, one inside wall still showing the original construction of mud and wattle. My brother and I used to sleep in the Oak Room, darkly panelled with a widely boarded floor and high ceiling. Wooden stairs led up to the room with the mud and wattle wall, and beside the stairs was a shelved cupboard room. At night when it was dark I can remember hearing my brother tapping against a hollow panel and saying hoarsely, 'Listen, can you hear the ghost coming?' But really he was pulling my leg and the house was friendly with no restless ghosts to disturb our peace!

When the war came my uncle joined the Pioneer Corps, being no longer on the Reserve, and he and my aunt temporarily left the manor. We had been given his polo ponies to look after and keep on the rough banks surrounding our house. Apart from the horse population we had chickens, pigs, goats, a cow and her calf, not forgetting at one time a ram, given to us by some Americans when they left our district.

The animals were mostly my department, and it was also my responsibility to feed and milk the cow before setting off on an eight-mile bicycle ride to school, and again do the milking in the evening after bicycling and walking up Leckhampton Hill, with all my 'prep'.

There were lovely mornings when our house and fields were bathed in early sunshine, and yet the cloud hung around the top of the hill, hiding the great rock of the Devil's Table perched above us. Down below, the mist filled the valley, leaving only the summits of Churchdown and Robin Wood Hill like islands standing alone in a white sea. Indeed, the abrupt edge of our banks looked as though they dropped away into cliffs, and one could easily imagine the surf beating against their feet far below. Then the mist would roll up from the vale, enveloping me in its dewy coldness, as I staggered back with a full milk pail.

As the wall of the ha-ha loomed out of mist ahead, I would swing the bucket up and on to the top, seeing that the dog did not pop his nose into the rich, warm froth on the top of the pail, while I was clambering over. Often, by the time I had strained the milk and put it to stand for skimming the next day, and then changed from dungarees to school tunic, the mist would again have rolled away. Sometimes I rode through foggy clouds along the tops of the hills to find the town and school below were bathed in sunshine, but more often I left the lovely weather at home to descend into the thin, cold fog still lingering in the valley.

By the afternoon the sun would have worked with its warmth to disperse the valley mist, but I was always glad to climb back home in the evening to our superior and solitary position.

In the holidays I helped on farms, apart from doing our own work at home. No doubt this hard physical work toughened me up for other exertions. In between time I rode our horses over the lovely natural countryside, jumping gates and walls that came in our way, providing that there was no farmer's crop that could be damaged in the field beyond. At that time I was passionately interested in farming and although I was only earning fourpence an hour, I dreamt that one day I would own great estates in England, or even enormous ranches in distant lands.

When I was riding, I would encourage the horses to jump any likely obstacle. I built some very rustic-looking fences in our field, and often while we were hauling up logs from the woods, with a pony and sledge, I would drop off a pole or two in places where I could later build a jump.

[3]

During the war I used to ride at Pony Club gymkhanas and charity shows, with the horses doing the events such as musical sacks, V.C. race, potato race and bending race, as well as the jumping! Nowadays jumping is much too specialized to risk one's best horse in a gymkhana event! At that time I used to ride to the shows, or if they were very far away I would share the expense of a cattle lorry with a friend.

After the war and the death of my father, Mother and I had to live in various places in order to keep the horses. It was more economical to carry the horses with our own transport, and by the time we had moved to Miserden in 1949 we owned a jeep and a two-wheeled horse trailer.

In this lovely part of the country, quite near to where we had lived during the war, we were able to start a home of our own again. This typical Cotswold house is on the estate of Wing-Commander and Mrs. Huntly Sinclair, and the history of these parts goes back to Saxon times. The church has a Saxon doorway and the village was mentioned in the Doomsday Book as Green Hampstead. When William the Conqueror came to England he promised to give castles and land to his followers.

One of his Norman barons, known as 'Le Musardier' (the poacher), although his real name was Haskard Musard, was given the castle at Green Hampstead and it was through a contraction of his name that the village changed to Miserden, and became the only place of this name in the world. Later the Fair Maid, Joan of Kent, inherited the castle from her father, and it is pleasant to think of Joan and her husband the Black Prince wandering through these same woods and valleys that we ride over now.

[4]

My uncle's house at Swindon, near Cheltenham

Miserden

Miserden House

Tosca being exercised on the lunging rein

Mother and I enjoyed the hard work involved to get our new home in running order, and meantime the horses were not neglected. Pauline Sykes had just arrived and immediately got into the stable routine to take over gradually the responsibility of the horses, until now, when anything she does not know about the feeding, health and travelling of show jumpers would not fill a postage stamp. Some people have a gift for looking after animals. Pauline certainly has it, but the work she does behind the scenes and the complete dedication of her time and energy to the horses would put off many young people who think that looking after horses is an easy job. It is most difficult to produce highly strung and sensitive animals in the pink of condition, especially when they are travelling long distances in a troublesome climate, with irregular hours and various changes of food and water. However, Paul always has the horses looking and feeling well, and their comfort and well-being comes before any thought for herself.

Just as the popularity of show jumping has grown with the public, I found that it absorbed more and more of my own time. I had first been abroad with the British team in 1947 and without thinking that show jumping would become so much of my life, my horses seemed to go on jumping higher and better as they took me further and further afield.

With this growth of the sport and the essential specialization to produce top-class results, of necessity life has had to change. From a jeep and trailer which could take two horses we now have a diesel lorry that can take four or even five. Paul has learnt to drive the lorry, which relieves me of a lot of the fatigue and saves my time.

In 1952, after the tragic motor accident to my mother, the whole running of the house had to be re-organized and the working out of these problems, with the financial ones and the complete uncertainty of the future, kept me busy enough to work off the shock. Now I have Paddy Bury to help me at home, and she has to deal with not only the friends and guests who come and stay, but also the housekeeping, first aid, the endless letters and all my typing, which in itself is a marathon job!

Our house has become a United Nations centre in miniature. Friends from all countries come, or send their children, relatives or friends' friends to learn a little of our life here. It is most interesting to see how language difficulty and nationality make no difference between the people who stay. Often they become better friends with a person from another country, than with someone of their own. Not only do people usually stay longer than they originally intended, but they also come back again. I am able to visit them in their homes and in this way I have been able to make good friends in many countries. I often wonder if nations would be so easily led to battle, if they knew more about the people they are supposed to fight. Sacrifices must always be made when living in a community, but life has never been promised as a wholly easy way, with oneself as the central attraction. I hope that the people who have met here in these unluxurious but pleasant surroundings, will always keep a happy memory of England and feel more tolerant of us and of each other. I know that from this exchange of guests I have learnt to admire much in these new friends, and in other people, that otherwise I would certainly have missed.

Apart from new languages and new recipes for cooking, with different music and games from other countries, the house has acquired quite an international flavour from the souvenirs that I have collected during my travels. Together with gifts brought by people visiting us from abroad, one can now find in various corners, an assortment of oddities varying from little Pennsylvania Dutch figures from America, a stuffed baby alligator from the alligator farm in Florida, a Spanish goat-skin bottle and a table from Algiers, to pictures from France, China and Spain to mention only a few of the countries. There is a Picasso which even I can interpret as being Don Quixote with the windmills of La Mancha, his home, in the background. This picture I was lucky enough to find for the equivalent of four shillings in Paris, and I get a thousand times that price in pleasure to see it hanging in the hall.

One day, the B.B.C. wrote to say that their televiewers would like to see where I lived, while I was not travelling the endless rounds of horse shows.

I had never really given the matter of television organization a thought until our home became Lime Grove itself when the 'At Home' programme was transmitted from these hitherto quiet Cotswold premises. As the great day approached, for the half-hour visit to our house, queues of cars arrived bringing busy people who wandered in and around as they wished, discussing the points of the house like horse dealers running down a likely purchase. Meantime the weather changed from snow to slight thaw, and then it froze to make the approaches to the house into sheets of rutted ice. By the time the ice had been spread with cinders and gravel there was plenty of scope for bringing the slushy grime on the soles of many feet, to decorate the floor of our stone hall.

The village had got used to our big diesel horsebox by now, but never have they seen such enormous ten-ton vans that descended on us and settled down in a snug cluster around the front of the house. One was the operating studio and control room, where the producers directed the whole proceedings and chose the picture from a choice of four as the programme was being transmitted. This complicated business had to be synchronized with the right volume of sound and the general directions given to all cameramen in order to rectify any mistakes or faults.

They brought to the village their own power, which was controlled in another of the vans. This supplied all the lighting effects apart from the power needed for the transmission. Electricians had erected scaffolding on some of the inside walls of the rooms to be televised, which supported the arc lamps necessary for a good picture. As none of the doors or hatches could be closed because of the heavy cables that ran through them, we ate our meals sitting in overcoats, rushing the food from the cooker to the dining-room, before the snow blowing through the back door could settle on the joint.

Our jumping paddock at the top of the village was filled with two large vans that did the actual transmitting. The weather was such that I could not have worked the horses there in any case, so they were welcome to the use of this bleak mountain top for their important mission.

Apart from these vans, there were the enormous lorries needed to bring the cameras and equipment. All this

[8]

excitement was keenly viewed by the local people, and even a large contingent from the village school, no doubt during the 'Current Events' lesson.

When all was more or less in place, with the heavy 'dollies' ready to wheel the heavier cameras from place to place, we started a rehearsal. We had roughly three run-throughs of parts of the evening's programme.

Two short film sequences were being shown during the half hour, the first being a film of Tosca and Flanagan out to grass on holiday with a few shots of my young horses Oberon and Brigadoon during training. I knew more or less what this film contained, but the second film was a completely 'dark horse'. It was supposed to have shots of Prince Hal when creating the Ladies European High Jump Record of 7 feet 3 inches at Brussels. However, from the verbal description of the film, I thought for certain that it would not turn out to be this competition, or even the show at Brussels. The jumps had been described exactly as those of Paris.

Luckily the film turned out to be the right one, although I had to do the commentary during the actual programme on the spur of the moment, viewing it on an indifferent monitor set, under the glare of the special lights. I was slightly foxed when, at the moment I saw Hal about to jump his 2 metres 20 centimetres record, the picture turned into a Dutchman on a white-faced horse cantering round the ring. Then the shot changed to Hal and me standing at attention, whip in salute, while the National Anthem was being played.

The other short film I had seen on a 16 mm. projector, just before the performance, so I knew roughly what to expect for the commentary. Even then, during the

[9]

actual performance, when the film was being relayed from London while I did the live commentary from the drawing-room, a neighbour's dog scuttled in to join the fun. The hackles went up on my three dogs, and I remembered just in time not to put my thoughts into words with the microphone ready to relay any sounds to the listening and watching world. By the time this crisis was over, I had had no time to draw attention to the original Algerian cap that I was wearing in the film. This cap had been brought home, after my short stay in the Sahara, to compete with the knitted fishermen's caps from Boulogne that Paul had bought for herself and the two other girls, Pam and Norma. When Paul appeared later in the programme, complete in her red, white and blue cap plus pom-pom, it would have been too complicated to explain its origin and our rivalry in headgear.

During the rehearsals, Oberon had played up to the cameras by making his low bow to the public, more often than required. Every time I turned my back on Oberon after he had done his bit by welcoming the audience to the stables, he would bow again, trying to show off and steal the thunder from Prince Hal. However, Hal was not in the least put out by this and played his part by gently taking small pieces of carrot from between my lips, like the true gentleman that he is.

The first run through was interrupted by an S.O.S. 'Quick, get some brandy, someone has slipped up in the yard and hurt his ankle.' As one of my French guests had brought us a bottle of 'Napoleon' for Christmas, I was able to administer this new remedy for sprains!

The time for the whole programme was so limited

that there could be no delay between the moves. During rehearsals the cameras had to be moved experimentally to find the best angles and places. This took a great deal of time and patience, especially when the camera had to follow one around the room, and across the hall. From the hall to the drawing-room, a ramp had to be built to wheel the heavy camera up the step into the alcove. The men then silently manœuvred it round the corner and through the door, with only an inch to spare on either side.

I had been quite lucky to get home from London before these final rehearsals, for not only was the weather bad, but the car had decided not to start that morning. In the country anyone will go out of their way to lend a hand or give a tow to a motorist in distress, but in big cities life is more impersonal, people are inclined to look the other way if they see a girl cranking a car without success! Eventually a kind person took pity on me, and with lengths of blind cord, which kept breaking, we towed the car round and round the square until she reluctantly fired, picked up, and spluttered into life. It would have been difficult for Hywel Davies, who was introducing my home to the viewers, had I not got back in time. The situation might have arisen where he opened the front door and said to the cameras, 'I am sorry we find that Miss Smythe is not at home, so we return to the studios for twenty-nine minutes' interlude.'

As it was, we were all in our places when the producer shouted, 'Stand by and silence, the programme starts in thirty seconds from now.' I felt as though I was just going into the ring to jump a Grand Prix course. Then the silence was broken by, 'Relax for a moment, the other programme is overrunning'. A moment or two later we began.

It all went so quickly that the time taken seemed like five minutes. The dogs followed me about like shadows so much so that Windy gave a yelp of displeasure when a camera man tried to stop her coming into one picture! Fina la Ina, the Lucas terrier puppy, hid under the sofa at one moment, pouncing out on the feet that passed. This was just the moment when I was talking to Hywel Davies, and suddenly out of the corner of my eye I saw a man crawling on his hands and knees behind a chair. Then I felt someone taking my hand and putting it on the arm of my chair. Fina thought that this was a fine game of a man playing dogs with her, but I could not think what was happening. Apparently my hand had been too close to the hidden microphone which spoilt the sound, so the producer had sent word through the bush telegraph for my hand to be moved. Nobody knows what goes on behind the seemingly solemn interview on the screen!

I had scarcely picked up my guitar for the closing song when the programme was all over. However, I must have sung enough to merit a remark in a fan letter a day or two later, 'We hope that you will bring back a gold medal from the Olympic Games, yours sincerely . . . PS. The gold medal will not be for singing.'

For the rest of the week the postman must have thought that Christmas had come round again, and at the week-end the village tree was as busy as Piccadilly Circus in rush hour. Our village being a dead end, all cars have to turn back either round the petrol pumps or the tree. We hoped that Miss Timms had done great trade that

Sunday afternoon, but between matins and evensong she had only been asked for two gallons of petrol.

A television interview in a studio does not bring nearly such repercussions. It is far more impersonal and after you have said your piece nobody notices if you melt away. In France the preparation is most amusing to watch. A small bar is usually set up in one corner, where the victims of the programme are encouraged to have an apéritif. While they are relaxing for a moment, the rest of the studio appears to be in chaos.

I have never rehearsed or been warned of the type of questions before an interview there. Suddenly frantic gestures from the producer summon me in front of the cameras and rapid questions in French are fired off in quick succession. Helped by the strengthening aperitif, it is extraordinary how people seem to cope quite easily with the replies, and the programme is finished with little effort involved.

During the jumping show in Paris, some of the events were televised. The first time that this was relayed to Britain, one half-hour had been allotted for the programme. As the whole evening is dedicated to the jumping, time is immaterial. So it happened that day, when instead of the exciting finals to the Puissance with horses jumping huge fences of well over 6 feet, the cameras came into play between two events. Lads were seen nonchalantly moving fences, raising bars and lowering them again and then moving the fence a yard or two. Someone in a homburg hat would arrive with a measuring stick and find that the height was wrong, so great gesticulations would follow. Riders were walking vaguely about the ring, stepping out the distances between

[13]

the doubles and then shrugging their shoulders hope-
lessly. A rider imagines a jump is far more difficult
without the horse between his knees. Then there is the
psychological fact that if one makes a great fuss about
the difficulties, the other competitors may get anxious.
A more important matter is that if one brags about the
simplicity of a course, the horse may decide to make its
rider an object lesson, in front of his friends, and reveal
the unseen difficulties hitherto overlooked. Some of the
experienced champions walked round the course, with a
deadpan expression covering their thoughts and working
out exactly the best way to win. Others just stood in
group and gossiped, making the delay a social occasion
with a chance to talk to their friends in the freedom of the
ring, rather than competing in the crush by the ring
side.

All this *va-et-vient* did not help the commentator to
fill in his time. Although both Dorian Williams and
Bill Allenby have all the experience for their commentating on show jumping, this lack of action while the
B.B.C.'s valuable time was ticking away must have been
exasperating. Eventually a few preliminary rounds
were jumped.

The next time the Paris jumping was televised the
programme was a great success. Viewers saw an exciting
event with horses jumping in a speed competition.
The cameras were sited below the jumps, getting a 3-D
effect of the leap over an enormous fence and almost out
of the screen and into the room. This effective way of
televising was again cut short for viewers, as the final was
jumped after midnight.

However exciting the actual competition may be, a

camera cannot capture that unique feeling of crowd atmosphere, that can so easily influence the competitors. In certain countries whistling can be encouraging, whereas in others it is definitely a noise of disapproval. The American crowd in Harrisburg had been very kind to the British team with their enthusiasm and support. Still, I was rather worried as I brought Prince Hal out of the ring after the final win in his unbeaten run through the show, when I heard whistling above the applause. This, I was kindly assured, was a way of expressing their approval!

With individuals, the cameras can give a far more true picture of a person's character than the opinion formed from the hearsay of gossip columns. In order to make news, there may be an inclination to hint at bitter rivalry within a team, whereas in actual fact only friendship and will-to-win exist. Like this, any spark of jealousy can be ignited and fanned in the search for sensation. In the same way divorce hits the headlines while a happy marriage is not 'exciting' enough for comment.

It is extraordinary how easily people believe reports often written by those not well versed in the true facts of their story. People have come up to me and said, 'I see you are going to South Africa.' With some surprise I have replied, 'Am I? I did not know anything about it.' Followed by the firm assurance, 'Oh, yes, I read it in the paper!' Perhaps one is expected to lead a life influenced by one's destiny as told by the stars.

Once something has appeared in a paper, be it false or inaccurate, it is difficult to rectify the harm. Even if the truth appears later, the original account has been absorbed by the reading public. The responsibility of those who write is summed up in the famous lines from *The Rubá'iyát of Omar Khayyám:*

> The moving finger writes; and, having writ,
> Moves on: nor all thy piety nor wit
> Shall lure it back to cancel half a line,
> Nor all thy tears wash out a word of it.

When the camera is relaying a horse jumping, the rider seldom realizes that his changes of expression can be so closely recorded, or even that he is actually being televised. Of necessity the cameras are remote, and only a telephoto lens can bring such a close-up on to the screen. Even in a television interview one can get so interested in a good discussion with somebody, that the fact is forgotten that an invisible audience is listening, and the cameras are recording.

In the United States, I had an interview when I was staying in the Middle West. Without briefing, I was sat on a sofa with my interviewer who was interested in finding out the European outlook and life on our side of the world. Our conversation had left the horses far behind after the first three minutes. The half-hour fled by with our discussion obviously interesting those who heard it, for they wrote and asked for repeats of the programme. By the time I had expressed my sincere but not extremely knowledgeable views on British problems that interested the American public, the next person on the programme was pacing up and down behind the camera. He had caught an enormous Muscavi fish weighing 41 lb. and there it was on the scales so that there could be no argument about the fisherman's story.

The Americans have a very efficient secret service in

order to get T.V., radio or newspaper interviews with
their victims. I had no planned schedule of events while
I was travelling around, in fact I lived by faith and the
kindness of the people I met. In spite of this the Press
seemed to anticipate my movements and I had interesting
talks at every place I visited. The local towns, especially in the Middle West, were always ready to question
their picture of our life at home. Often they had formed
imaginary ideas because they had not had a chance to
meet an ordinary English citizen. The deepest and most
pleasing impression that I was given was the respect and
idolatry that all, from the housewife to the business man,
held for our Queen and Sir Winston Churchill.

Great people like these command international fame,
without the necessity of publicity. However, it is
terrifying that television can make quite ordinary characters become household words. Then there are others
who find themselves thrust into prominence through this
medium, in spite of a preference to remain out of the
public eye.

So much for the effect that television has on our lives,
both at the camera end and also at the viewing end, where
there is a chance of becoming a slave to the set, ignoring
visitors, relations, work, games, the garden and the
hundred and one useful things that should be done about
the house!

I enjoyed my introduction to the working side of our
'At Home' programme. I also enjoyed the preliminary
organization, interviews and preparation, apart from the
interesting people that I met; in fact it was an experience
that I would not have missed for anything.

When it was all over, no sooner had I listened to the

echoes of the vans disappearing down Daneway Hill, than I began thinking that I would escape from the back-wash caused by the plunge of T.V. splashing abroad our quiet life in this backwater of the Cotswolds.

So I left the continuous ringing of the telephone and the accumulation of the hundred and one jobs that I had not done. I left the scrubbing of the flag stones in the hall, and I left the ice and snow still lying around our home. I journeyed to the ice and snow of Switzerland, where I hoped to do some writing for five days, in the tranquillity of the mountains.

CHAPTER 2

Downhill

MY father, having been brought up in Switzerland, had told me many stories about his life
there. He had been in a bob-sleigh team, one
of the fastest of the winter sports. He skated, skied and
above all—climbed mountains.

At home, his study was surrounded with pictures of
formidable mountains, the Matterhorn, the Eiger, the
Dents du Midi, Mont Blanc and many other fierce and
jagged peaks. We heard how he had to bivouac on the
Matterhorn for a night, with terrible electric storms
raging around him, and how the mountains can change
their mood from a friendly welcome to a furious passion
against the intruders of their domain. I was absorbed in
the stories of Whymper and Mallory and read of their
feats and battles with the elements as soon as I was strong
enough to extract my father's heavy mountaineering
books from the library. In fact it was from Guido Rey's
description of a night on the Matterhorn that I learnt my
first few words in French. One of the climbers asked
the guide when the storm would abate, and his reply had
been, 'Qui sait? On ne peut pas dire'.

I was stupid enough never to speak a word of a foreign
language to my father, although he could speak fluent
French and German. I imagined, from being brought up
during the war, that I would never go abroad, and that

anyway I did not want to make a fool of myself talking French when I could express myself and be understood much more easily in English. I regretted this later when I found myself in foreign countries, and unable to speak even the French I had learnt for the school certificate. So, since then, I have had to work doubly hard at languages, as without them, one is completely handicapped when meeting and talking to people from abroad.

I longed to go to Switzerland more than anything, and I was eighteen when the chance came. Some friends, with whom we had stayed at the beginning of the war, the Mackintosh and Drummond Hay families, asked me to join a party they were taking to Zermatt for ski-ing. They were all terrific skiers and I had always wanted to try this exciting sport.

When Sheena Mackintosh's letter arrived, Mother generously said that I must take the opportunity to have ten days in Switzerland. At the time, we were working very hard and living in one room at the Blathwayt, by the racecourse above Bath. I did not want to leave Mother to cope alone while I was away, but she insisted that she could manage.

Ever since I was very small, I have been a regular contributor to the Post Office Savings Bank. With sixpences and shillings gleaned from pocket money and kind relations, my account by then had attained double figures. Then with the horses winning an occasional profit over expenses at the local shows, I had accumulated enough to pay for this trip. So the Postmaster General lost my valuable support and with my money invested in a ticket for Switzerland, I set off to London to get the boat train from Victoria.

At work

At home

Hal, Windy, and Bliss

Christmas decorations!

Pauline Sykes, Norma Horsburgh, and Pamela Forrest with Oberon in the stable yard

The wild and woolly West at Miserden. Tosca, just up from her winter's rest

The back of the house

Most of the party were already in Switzerland, but a few of us were travelling out together. It was the first time I had really been abroad, except when I was about two and a half and had been taken for a summer holiday to Le Zoute on the Belgian coast.

By the time we had crossed the channel and settled for the night in the French train, we had sorted ourselves out in the carriages. I had a luggage rack to sleep in and three of the others had pulled the cushion part of the seats into the middle, making the whole floor into one big mattress. During the night I woke up to find I was nearly suffocated in the hot air that had risen to the top of the compartment. I struggled to open the window quietly, getting very black in the process. The train had stopped and I tried to muster some French to ask a passing porter where we were. Luckily the guard shouted 'Rheims' at that moment, and I went to sleep again dreaming of jackdaws on skis.

The next morning we were surrounded by wonderful snowy peaks. I had never thought that mountains could be so enormous and I was staggered by the size and height of the ranges towering above us. We wound up through the Lotschberg Pass, coming out on the mountains one stage higher after each spiral of tunnel. I remembered a Geography lesson when a dear old Scottish mistress had described this tunnel so clearly and then finished her lesson by saying in her soft brogue, 'And now, pass out quietly, girls.' We had proceeded to fall flat on our faces and anything but quietly! That had been at Seaford, when our school was evacuated from Wimbledon. Dorothy Tutin was one of the girls, although she was a little junior to me—eleven years old!

We arrived at Zermatt in the dark, just in time to change for the fancy dress party in honour of the New Year. The next day I started at the ski school in earnest. I had hired some boots and skis and managed to pack the boots out with layers of socks. Some kind person in England had lent me brown woollen trousers, that had been used as an air-raid warden's suit, specially designed for keeping out the cold in the shelters during the war. It was certainly very cold outside, so I wore my pyjama trousers under the ski trousers. That night I found my pyjamas had turned brown from the dye running out of the wet woollen trousers. I then realized why proper ski-ing clothes are waterproof, and an absolute necessity for a beginner like me, who spends half the time caked with snow from head to foot!

I could hardly concentrate on the morning's lesson, because of the lovely sight of the Matterhorn dominating the view from the the nursery slopes, pointing like a needle fang into the blue sky, proudly aloof from the other clusters of mountains.

By the afternoon, some of us thought ourselves good enough to start a little ski jumping. We abandoned our ski sticks and commandeered a jump about six inches high, built by the youngest of the village children. After attaining record distances of two feet or so, I made the mistake of trying to copy one of the under five's who had done a brilliant jump, and then stopped at the bottom of the slope with a 'Christi' turn. Instead of the slower and more controlled stem turn, with the backs of the skis well apart, and in the case of most beginners, the bottom and elbows stuck well out for extra balance, I tried the showy and classical turn with the skis together. Alas, my weight, balance and edges were wrong, although the spirit was willing and the inclination right. So instead of swishing round to an elegant stop, I turned head over heels, twisting my ankle in the process, and found myself on the steep slope with my head downhill and my feet and skis, looking in opposite directions, above me. I almost needed a table of logarithms to work out the answer to the problem of how to extract myself from this position.

I was very lame for a day or so, though this did not stop me ski-ing, as the tight boots give extra support to a swollen and black ankle. That next day, I came down the long mountain run, arriving at the bottom in excellent time because of my complete inability to stop or turn. I had taken most of the slopes straight, sitting down hard when an undue hazard loomed ahead. I really thought I was getting on famously until I tried the same run on the third day. By then my muscles were tired and I was trying too hard. I had been told that good skiers only fell forwards, so I was determined not to sit down. Sure enough I fell, and fell forwards, dislocating my thumb on the ski stick. This thumb from then on continued to dislocate itself at any inconvenient time, especially if I caught it on the horse's neck when riding. I often use the leverage of my thumb on the neck, in order to get more tension on the reins if a horse is pulling hard.

After this fall, I could not stand up for more than a moment. Every few yards I found myself buried in another snowdrift, then faced again the ghastly problem of working out how to extricate myself from the depths and getting into a mobile position again. It was as bad as trying to get a golf ball out of a bunker with a driver, and the more I struggled the more exhausted I became. In the end I longed just to lie and rest engulfed in snow, but then the wet cold would start to penetrate and I would redouble my efforts to struggle free.

Zermatt looked such a long way below me, and Castor and Pollux, the twin Zwillinge Mountains above, were laughing clouds of snow off their sides as they watched my antics.

The next day I forced my agonized feet into the un-relenting ski boots, and dragged myself back to the ski school. Here I learnt about relaxation with control and how one must always bend one's knees, to keep to the rhythm of the skis over the bumpy slopes. 'Arlvice niece bent', our guide would yell every other moment, as we rushed by out of control with straight legs and behinds stuck out, too often leaning back at the critical moment and coming to an abrupt halt, camouflaged in a cloud of snow, with the 'sitz stop'. 'And so', he would sigh as he sorted me out and unwound a tangle of limbs, skis and sticks.

What fun it all was, in spite of the blackest and most colourful bruises that I have ever had. The best part of all were the runs down from the heights, with the freedom of the great snow fields and the feeling that one was an explorer with the opportunity of marking the slopes with a gracefully curved or a dashing straight line, or perhaps mar the smoothness of the snow with two ugly and jerky ski tracks, pock-marked with holes from the various tumbles en route.

How I wished that I was good enough not to abuse this gift of snow, and to be able to explore glaciers and ski routes that would need expeditions of a day or more.

All this, with the Matterhorn always present, although absorbed in its own thoughts as the snow blew off its summit and into the heavens, like a volcano offering up its sacrifice and intercession in a plume of smoke. I was sad to leave the majesty of the mountains and I returned home to find England gripped in the Arctic conditions of 1947, with seventeen-foot drifts of snow but no facilities for making sport with it.

The next time I visited the mountains was for only four days, after a tough journey with Leona across France in the grip of winter. Leona, my grey mare, was going to her new owner, and after seeing her safely across France by goods train and into her comfortable stables in Switzerland, I left for the Bernese Oberland to try and remember the little ski-ing I had learnt during that week at Zermatt five years before.

I stayed in a chalet with a Swiss friend, Mimi Mylius, and her two small children. The first evening, I tried out my best Schwitzerdütsch when saying goodnight to the children. I got a quick reply to my 'Gute Nacht'. Robertli, her eight-year-old son, said, 'Gute Nacht, traüm süess, machs Bett nicht voll.' By the time the grownups' laughter had subsided, I had discovered that this was the usual goodnight to small children, meaning 'sweet dreams and don't wet your bed!'

The next day we went up the mountain to do a run down. We each took some cheese, Bündnerfleisch, the delicious dried meat that one cuts paper thin, and an orange, so that we could have a picnic in the sun.

The children skied very well, though being so light they did not get up a tremendous speed. I adopted my former tactics of going fast and straight, because I had little control, and now and then making a spectacular hole in the snow.

The four days I had then whetted my appetite for a week the following year, when I went to the ski school regularly to try and get some basic style and control.

More than in any other sport, there is in ski-ing a great risk of an accident. If anything goes wrong at a high speed, and the ski gets caught as one falls, some limb is bound to twist. However, there are also risks in everything one does, and even if every precaution is taken through life, there is still the danger of stepping under a bus or slipping on a banana skin. For me, the short holiday was a complete tonic, for not only did I get very fit, but I absorbed the mountain sun at a most needed time during the winter. From the point of view of riding, I am sure that ski-ing gives one added dash and confidence. The quick decisions that one must make on skis help towards an alertness and a co-ordination between thought and movement. Apart from this, one feels so well in the crisp and dry mountain air.

When I first went away, I spent the quiet evenings in the chalet knitting, while gossiping to Swiss friends who joined us for some coffee. I used to enjoy the tranquillity of those evenings but now I have to take advantage of this more peaceful week* in the year to get some writing done! With the temptation of ski-ing the next day, I can set myself the task of writing so many pages. If I do not get enough written I cannot ski the next day, but so far this has never happened.

With a time limit in which work must be finished, it is

* This chapter was written during a week's holiday in February 1956.

amazing how much one can do especially with an incentive—no work, no sport!

Chalet life is very pleasant and quite different from staying in an hotel. Sometimes families share a chalet, with the children combining school work and their winter ski-ing. Early in the morning I would hear the children rattling the boards overhead as they energetically got dressed. They had to get some lessons and homework done, before going to ski school at 10 a.m. When I heard them getting up I only needed to open one eye and see that the huge puffy eiderdown was in place, then steal another half-hour's sleep.

By the time I managed to muster the courage to get out of bed and shut the window, I was very ready to collect a cup of coffee. Then before leaving for the ski school, I would have a quick scrounge around for my lunch of cheese and an apple, taking care to put the solid apple in a different pocket from the place I had bruised the day before. I invariably fell on the apple, especially if the ground was hard and icy, so by lunch time it would be partly pulped as well as leaving great bruises on me. The cheese was a pretty pink colour as it was mixed with ham and called *Schinkechäes*, or before I could pronounce this word, I would think of it as 'stinkin' cheese'.

Then there is the agony of lacing the heavy boots on poor feet that are not hardened or used to such torture treatment, but the boots are a necessity and once one is acclimatized they become part of the mountain life.

On a sunny morning the peaks of the mountains catch the first glow of the early sun, and the rays steal down the mountain sides, sparkling the snow until the warmth reaches the skiers on the nursery slopes. The gay colours of the skiers' jackets and caps make a gay contrast against the white snow. By 10 a.m. the pupils of the ski school of every age, type and nationality are waiting in groups for the guides. Then the *Skilehrer* arrive to take charge of their classes. These instructors are all excellent skiers, brought up with the tradition of the mountains, and probably having started ski-ing as soon as their parents could put them into ski boots. By the time they leave school they have become expert skiers, and ready to take the difficult *Skilehrer* examination, which of course includes the fluent use of several languages. Many have won high-class races and jumping events and all have adventured over the mountains and glaciers getting experience of every condition of snow and weather.

Some of the children living in the mountains have to ski to school, so they can use their skis as easily as other children can ride a bicycle. No wonder we lowlanders, who perhaps ski for a week or two each year, are at a disadvantage when competing at ski-ing with the mountain people. They live on skis, which are a necessary part of their lives during the winter, from the time they are out of the cradle.

During the summer many of the instructors go mountaineering as guides to tourists. This tough and busy life does not give them much time for rest or a holiday. Most of them are small farmers as well, with a few cows which must be cared for between their other work. During the summer, hay has to be collected from high up the slopes for winter feed. In the months when the cows can graze on the mountains, they must be watched to see that they do not stray too far or fall down some precipice and get hurt.

Other guides may be carpenters or builders in their spare time, or even a plumber, like Toni Seiler. This triple Olympic gold-medallist, sensation of the 1956 winter games at Cortina, managed to find time apart from his work to become the genius skier of his generation. The three events he won, the Cross-country, Downhill and Slalom races, are each so different in character that his great triple feat is almost unique in the history of the sport.

It is probably this very hard work and tough life that makes the guides into such genuine, kind and charming people with great character. It would be difficult for them to get spoilt even by the rich tourists, when after ski-ing or mountaineering they are perhaps entertained in the hotels by the visitors and then they have to go back home to do the milking and other chalet chores! Again, in the morning, there is the same routine before appearing at the ski school to teach the classes.

Under the expert tuition of these guides, the motley and varied stream of tourists and holidaymakers of all nationalities who come throughout the winter and spring, learn how to get more pleasure and co-operation from their skis. Following the bobbing tassel on the guide's gay woollen cap, and seeing his graceful, easy movements as he glides down the mountain with complete control, gives confidence to any follower. I found it more difficult, when following a not-so-expert member of the class, who fell in front of me. Apart from the difficulty of suddenly having to circumnavigate a floundering body, I felt that perhaps this part of the mountain must be difficult and I was bound to fall, too!

That morning I had trudged up to the top of the

nursery slopes with the line of other skiers shouldering their skis, and either making use of the ski sticks to walk with or putting them over the other shoulder to support the ends of their skis. During the two-hour lesson, I found no time to look up and admire the lovely mountains above, for I needed all my concentration on the job in hand and my skis under foot.

Just at the moment when my confidence was ebbing, a good class of tiddlers, all aged under ten, came flying by not noticing our clumsy efforts. They were led by a young guide who was ski-ing with the youngest member of the class held safely between his knees, as the child had become tired before they reached this part of their run. Thinking how easy it looked when seeing such small children ski-ing so fast, I immediately tried to emulate their neat turns over a bump, and promptly sat down— on the apple in my pocket. My guide's tanned and wrinkled face looked worried, until he saw I was all right, then he smiled behind his sun glasses and demonstrated how I turned and why I had fallen. It did look very funny.

Once school was over, I rushed to catch the cable car to the top of the mountain. We all crowded in, squashing skis, sticks and people into the minute space. A bell rang and the square car soared up the cable towards the top of the mountain.

We pressed our faces against the window, making misty circles on the cold glass, as we watched the village retreating below us. Then on the sheer mountain side I saw a chamois standing camouflaged against a rocky crag. There were tracks of these mountain goats on the snow which led to the pine woods clinging perilously to the mountain side. I heard some of the expert skiers discussing the possibility of a route down this side of the mountain. To me it looked like suicide.

In a few moments more we reached the summit, and I had an excited feeling, anticipating the ski run down. I get just the same sort of feeling waiting before a jumping competition. We crowded out of the car into the cold wind and the brilliant sun reflecting off the bright white snowfields. The village we had just left was thousands of feet below us, and I felt very small and insignificant as I looked at the regiments of powerful mountains around us.

Starting down the great snowfield with the freedom of space, I felt like an explorer, first to mark the beauty of the snow. My thoughts were interrupted by my spectacular fall into the soft depths with clouds of powdery snow being shot into the air.

It is extraordinary how little damage one can do when having a fearful fall, although another time may prove less lucky. Further down the run, the cold, from the snow I had collected around my neck and middle, was wearing off with the exhilaration of speed. We stopped for a moment and I realized that my knees were feeling tired.

On the next stage I tried to remember to keep my skis together. I thought I was going well until I looked down and saw that not only were my skis far from being together, but also the tips were wobbling in a most unstable manner. I felt horror in my heart and I could not get them together before some icy ridges, but somehow we got safely past this hazard and began to zig-zag down the bumps. All went well as we turned smoothly over the crest of each bump and I began to feel the rhythm and balance that one can also get with a well-schooled horse. As we hit an icy patch, I found I could skid without losing balance. It was wonderful, until I began to experiment with my weight and I caught the wrong edge of the ski! It was no different from experimenting to find the best balance for a horse and even then one usually learns from mistakes.

Down to the station just as the train was coming in, and in time to compete with the crowd in getting skis on the rack and a portion of a seat in the train. Everyone looked happy whether they were tanned old hands or white-faced newcomers. People were smoking black cigarettes and I brought out my cheese and bruised apple to eat on the way up. Someone passed round a flask of Kirsch saying, 'Come on, drink some of this it will give you *vorlage*.' This meant that we should go flying down the mountain leaning well forward with 'soft knees', in a confident and relaxed mood.

Soon it was time to get stiffly out of the train, lace up my boots and start down the other side of the mountain. I was tempted to stay in the sun, listening to the accordion and the yodelling, but it was getting late. Snow was blowing off the mountain tops and the cold of the evening was freezing the snow and making the tracks very icy.

Before I was half-way down, I looked back to watch the sun setting and the mountains changing colour in the evening glow. All was quiet except for the crackling swish of the late skiers on the icy *piste*. Dusk came quickly as I got back to the chalet, to undo my frozen bindings and tramp up the squeaky wooden stairs into the warmth. After a bath and some coffee, I could sit down and write, inspired by the fluency of that last run down.

Having twisted myself twice on a mountain side, I have

experienced being taken down on a luge by the 'body-snatchers'. I had been warned, that in the case of injury, it was really better to wait for a luge, the low flat sledge they use, rather than accept any offers of rescue work by helicopter. Apparently the type of helicopter available was open to various hazards from temperature and altitude, making a rescue trip a fifty-fifty chance of even arriving at a hospital. On the other hand by luge, in spite of cold and discomfort, one was at least reasonably sure of completing the trip down the mountain.

The first time that I hurt myself I was strapped on the luge and taken down by two of the men who stamp out the *piste*, which is the track prepared for the skiers, as the regular body-snatchers were not about. The victim is tied down with the head to the front, so that he is travelling looking at the sky, or the mountains above with his own feet in the foreground. Like this, he is unable to see the precipices down which he is about to descend and so panic, scream or faint with fear.

We had a terribly steep bit to get down, so one man held a rope to help steady the luge from the back. In front I could not see what was going on, but just when we seemed to be going down a perpendicular, icy piece, and my feet were way above my head, the man acting as a brake to the luge lost a ski. He went flat on his face, luckily still holding the rope attached to the luge. At the same time he was trying to reach for his ski and stop the man at the front, who was concentrating intently on the descent so had not heard the shemozzle behind. Eventually I was halted at a hazardous angle and the ski was retrieved. When all had been sorted out, we continued the cold and bumpy journey down.

I can imagine and feel for the agony of anyone with a broken limb, having to use this method of transport. The next time I damaged myself was not so bad, and I waited in the sun for my rescuers. After a long time the luge appeared, but continued down the mountain without picking me up. It already had a body strapped on to it, with ski boots ominously sticking out at the end of the rug.

We had been watching the good and not-so-good skiers coming down the stretch of snow above us, and disappearing over the edge of a steep run that led down towards the first huts on the mountain side. My attention was caught by a tall and graceful figure ski-ing fast and easily down the *piste*, and to my surprise he made a detour and came to a halt where I was sitting. He lent over towards me and started chanting a little *Schwitzerdütsch* love song and then invited me to ski down with him to the valley below. Sadly I told him that my spirit was willing but my knee was not so co-operative. 'You're injured,' he exclaimed. 'Why, I have the very thing to cure you,' and with a flourish he produced a flask from his pocket. It was reminiscent of hunting, when a flask is produced from a hunting coat pocket, in a moment of crisis. In the flask was *Bätzi*, the home-brewed firewater that evaporates as it touches the lips. He insisted that I should take a tot and no doubt if I had then smoked a cigarette, it would have burned with a blue flame, providing that I had not already blown up as I struck the match!

My teeth stopped chattering as I felt the *Bätzi* glow through me, and I was better prepared to stand the throbbing of my knee and the increasing cold. My friend and his flask disappeared down the mountain, flying smoothly and easily with his skis together, as wafts of yodelling were carried back to me from his willowy figure diminishing into the distance.

Again a long wait, with the sun slipping behind the mountains, leaving us in their cold shadow. At last I saw another luge, but again it had a body strapped on to it. I obviously should have hurt myself further up the mountain, in order to get luge priority!

I called out in despair, 'Is there another luge coming?' The man taking the luge could only speak Swiss German, and this taxed my knowledge of languages too much. I could only think of various German songs that I had heard with charming words that mean 'How is it possible that I can lose thee, my heart's delight', or 'I know not what e'er the reason that I am so sad', even 'Blue is the flower called Forget-me-not', which did not help much in the situation.

However, with a careful selection of these words, helped by gesticulations, he realized that I wanted to get down the mountain. Suddenly he bent down and began unstrapping the body lying silent and still on the luge. With horror, we tried to stop him taking off this body, with its ashen grey face peeking through a balaclava helmet. He was quite unmoved at our protests, and merely said 'Nei, nei,' as he unwrapped the blankets showing the man with his hands crossed on his chest over a hot water bottle. At this moment, to my astonishment, the corpse leapt to his feet, gathered up his skis and trotted off into the snow. We learnt later that he was a German who had lost his nerve on the way down, and so firmly took his skis off and sent a message for the

[35]

luge to take him down, at the same time vowing that he would never again participate in this dangerous sport. He was a wise man to get a hot water bottle organized too, for the luge is not the warmest method of coming down a mountain, and after a long descent the victim might even have frost bite to add to his troubles.

I was duly battened down in his place and hurtled off down the mountain. The efficiency of the man with the luge was terrific as we whisked down precipices and over icy patches, but in spite of his great concentration I did hear him giggle once when he heard my attempts at yodelling. With that jolting journey I understood why yodelling was so much easier than straight singing. Perhaps one day there will be super-sprung luges for the use of badly damaged victims!

This was not the only use for luges, as we used a small one for all the carting of shopping and luggage and as the quickest way of getting down to the village.

One night we luged into the village, shouting 'Achtung' to warn anybody unwise enough to get in our way. There was a ski jumping competition under floodlights, and we went to watch the best competitors from neighbouring villages. After some good jumping in the competitions, some of the *Skilehrer* gave a display for fun. They were in a crazy mood and came whisking over the jump in pairs and then as a 'follow my leader', with at least two in the air at the same time. To finish with came the most spectacular jump when the lights were put out. We saw two flaming torches rushing down towards the jump, held by the guide as he took off, making a perfect arc through the air to land safely in the semi-darkness.

Paul with Tosca and Hal

Severe concentration during the ski-school slalom race

On the Mannlichan before the start of the *Sunday Times Cup* race. Needless to say, I was not a competitor

After this great display we went to get a meal in one of the cafés. I was lucky enough to be given a ride down piggy-back by one of the skiers. I think I would have felt much safer on a horse.

For supper we had a Fondue Bourguignonne. A casserole dish half filled with olive oil was placed in the middle of the table with a flame under it to keep it hot. We had dishes of raw steak cut into cubes, also pieces of kidney, sausage and liver. With a long-handled fork we selected a piece of meat and dipped it into the hot oil. If we wanted it well done we held it in the oil longer than for a 'rare' mouthful of steak. If one burnt one's mouth with the sizzling piece, there was delicious sparkling Swiss wine to quench the fire.

The famous Swiss Fondue is made from cheese, a proportion of which must be Emmenthal. When the hot cheese is simmering in the casserole, the diners dip pieces of bread into the dish, twisting them round to break off the strings of cheese, like spaghetti, that stretch between the dish and the bread as it is popped into the mouth. Delicious though this is, it is very heavy, and even energetic dancing cannot always work off the effects of a cheese fondue. In fact indigestion would probably be the result.

During the meal I heard stories of the mountains and of the closeness between life and death when one is trespassing on their territory. As I walked back to the chalet in the stillness of the moonlight, the mountains looked remote but friendly and it was hard to imagine them in a different mood.

During the night, I was excited at the thought of more ski-ing the next day, and I had a dream. I was climbing

D [37]

up to the top of the run leading to the jump platform, but before I turned properly to face downhill, my skis started slipping. I hardly had my balance as gravity and the steep slope precipitated me towards the platform. As I took off, straight into space, both the flaming torches in my hands went out. Falling in total darkness, I braced myself for the crash as I landed. When it came, I awoke with a start to find myself on the floor.

After I had remade my bed, I read *Ozymandias* to give my thoughts a change of scenery.

CHAPTER 3

'America, my New Found Land'

I

SOUTH TO FLORIDA

AFTER the shows had finished, it seemed a pity to use my return ticket home before I had seen a little more of America. My friend and rival from the show jumping competitions, Shirley Thomas, and her parents, kindly invited me to drive to their home at Ottawa. I saw Prince Hal and Tosca, in the good care of Pauline, start off on their long journey back to England. Shirley and I took her father's car and left Toronto, on a grey November day, for the three-hundred-mile drive home. Some of the country we passed through was typical Red Indian territory that I had imagined in my childhood, with lakes and rocky hills covered with scrub. I pictured canoes snooping out of the creeks and wooded hills hiding wig-wams and the Indian squaws with their families. In actual fact the Indians had not lived as far north as this, and had only travelled through these parts when hunting and fishing.

The drive to Ottawa passed quickly with Mr. Thomas's black Cadillac eating up the miles of road. It was my first experience of driving a car with power steering, which for parking made this big car as handy as a bicycle.

In some of the American cars another luxury that intrigued me was the telephone connected by radio, so that we could ring our friends while driving along. We had already had great fun with the telephone in Bill Hanson's car. It had been of the greatest use when we could not find a friend's house. We rang them and described the road that we were driving along. While we spotted the landmarks they told us whether to go right or left until we arrived at their front door.

However, another time we arrived at a house to find no light in the hall, so we telephoned from the car and the friends duly answered. While we were talking to them one of us got out and rang the front door bell. The person on the telephone then said, 'I can hear your door bell ringing, shall I wait while you answer it?' and the friend replied, 'How clever of you to hear, yes, do you mind holding on a moment.' They arrived at the door to find all of us there in fits of laughter.

On another occasion we rang our hosts as we turned into their drive. Assuming a tough American accent, one of us said, 'State Police, emergency call, say, have you seen a grey Cadillac believed to be travelling in your direction. This is a stolen vehicle, containing four convicts escaped from the Penitentiary.' By this time we were slowly driving towards the house and an anxious white face suddenly appeared at the window. The face disappeared and back from the other end of the phone came the reply, 'Yeah, a Cadillac is coming towards the house now.' 'Keep them talking,' we replied. 'We will be right along, and watch out for guns.' The next moment our host came cautiously out of the back door, and found us helpless, with only the phone in hand and no guns.

After an interesting time in Ottawa seeing the city, and also having the honour of meeting the Governor, Vincent Massey, Shirley and I decided to leave the snow and go south to Pennsylvania, where I had been invited to go hunting with some friends I had made during the shows. We left the comfort of Twin Gates Farm at nine in the morning, and Shirley's blue Oldsmobile 88 made little of the slippery roads, and the blizzard that was blowing at the time. We headed south to the St. Lawrence River, which we crossed at the Thousand Islands bridge, where I had to renew my visitor's permit at the Customs.

In Canada I had found that snow does not paralyse traffic, as here, and the drivers are used to these conditions with their cars fitted with special tyres to minimize skidding risks. Once we were in the States we stopped for a quick lunch of hamburgers and ice-cream. The drug stores are a great advantage when driving long distances. Without wasting a moment one can have a hot-dog or hamburger, and be able to choose from a variety of ice-creams, with any flavour, colour or consistency.

Further south we passed through Syracuse, where I spotted a shop sale. As I was not equipped for a long journey after the shows, I bought a couple of gaily coloured shirts and a cowboy belt, for a dollar or two. Some of the towns we passed through had already started their Christmas decorations. In the dusk at Scranton we saw a pretty Christmas tree covered with fairy lights.

After a quick dinner, we drove for another hour or so, until we were tired from our drive of more than four

hundred miles that day. At the next suitable motel, we
stopped and paid for a cabin for the night. These motels
are ideal when one has long distances to cover, for they
are practical and inexpensive. A few of the larger ones
have restaurants attached, but this is unimportant. The
car is parked outside the cabin, and one is free to drive off
in the morning, collecting a cup of coffee or breakfast on
the road.

We had stopped in the Pennsylvania Dutch country,
and the next morning when we started in the sun, we
drove through wooded hills until we came to the Delaware Water Gap. With a view of the lake and the
autumn colours of the wooded valleys in the sun, we
stopped for coffee and acquired some souvenirs. I found
a wooden plate, engraved with the motto, 'If you wish to
be happy for one hour, get intoxicated; or for three days,
get married; or for eight days, kill your pig and eat it; or
for ever, learn to hunt and fish.' So we continued on our
way down the lovely river to Bethlehem, and further
inland to Chester County, our promised hunting
ground.

After seeing the two barns, or establishments, full of
horses in the charge of my friend Betty Bosley, we went
to her bungalow. As we arrived in the dark, a skunk ran
out of the wood-pile, frightened by the lights of the car.
This was the first time I had seen one of these little black
and white pests, and luckily I have yet to suffer from the
consequences of the smell. A skunk looks rather like a
squirrel, and when it is frightened it lifts its tail and squirts
an evil-smelling liquid at the object of its fear. This
liquid is penetrating and clinging, and if one's clothes are
touched it is almost impossible to get rid of the smell.

I knew of one man who sold his car for next to nothing, because he had run over a skunk, and after this, the smell in the car was unbearable.

The next day we had a great time hunting with the Unionville, and we met some of the charming people who hunt regularly with this excellent pack of foxhounds. Another day we drove down to Maryland over the Cono-wingo Dam. We found the course used in the race for the Maryland Hunt Cup, one of the highest steeple-chase honours for amateur riders to win in America. Some of the formidable and solid posts and rails are five-foot obstacles, not to be brushed through lightly by the race-horses! I think that I would prefer to race over our point-to-point fences rather than gallop full speed on an excitable thoroughbred at these 'fall enticers'. Nearby we were shown round Alfred Vanderbilt's Sagamore stud farm and I saw Native Dancer, one of the most famous of American horses, and his dam, Geisha, a grey mare. There were also two valuable stallions standing there. The most impressive part of the construction was a quarter-mile covered gallop around the outside of the central stables. The horses could be worked in any sort of weather either indoors when necessary, or out on the racecourse nearby, which was presumably maintained for private use. Apart from this, there were separate establishments for stallions, mares, horses in training and young stock. This busy day finished with the theatre in Philadelphia, seeing *Porgy and Bess*.

On the drive home, after a late supper of waffles, eggs and bacon and maple syrup, Betty told us of an exciting experience that she had had a little time before. She had been warned not to drive home after a party, alone and late at night. However, she had work to do in the morning and she thought that the thirty miles between Philadelphia and her home were not far enough to merit staying the night. While she was driving home she was thinking of the warning that her host had given her, and gradually she realized that she was being followed by another car. When she went fast, the car behind went fast, but when she went slowly it also went slowly, and refused to pass her. As this continued she began to feel frightened, and drove faster and faster, but the other car always followed. Tearing around corners at breakneck speed, suddenly she felt the panic of fear as she realized she had a flat tyre. Somehow she managed to pull into the side of the road and stop, and the other car shot past her and to her horror pulled up a little way in front. As she sat trembling in the driving seat, she saw the doors of the other car open and three coloured men stagger out. They looked drunk and dangerous, and she realized that here, alone in the country, a shout could not bring help. Also she realized that if she locked herself in the car, the windows could easily be broken. With sudden inspiration, she jumped out of the car and shouted to them, 'Say, you guys, that sure is kind of you to stop and help a girl in distress, I've got a flat tyre and I haven't a clue how to change the wheel.'

They hesitated for a moment and then two of them lunged forward, but the third, who seemed to be older, stopped them from touching her. He said, 'I guess if the lady thinks we all are gentlemen, we can all be of some help.' So he stood over the other two, who were made to change the wheel although they were muttering under their breath. After this, Betty got into the car and thanking them profusely drove home. She also thanked her lucky stars that she was not the victim of one of the seven nightly murders averaged in Philadelphia.

The next morning Shirley and I drove off to New York to do some Christmas shopping. Although we left early we expected to be there in good time, because after crossing the magnificent Delaware Memorial Bridge, the turnpike covered the whole distance through New Jersey to New York. We had been warned that the speed limit was 60 m.p.h., but the temptation of this straight and open road was too much. Before we had gone four miles we were 'copped', and had to pay the speeding fine of a dollar per mile per hour of excess speed. The cop could not have been more polite or charming, but it did not make the delay less expensive as we were taken to the nearest police station to pay the fine, before returning to the car to continue at a steady 60 m.p.h.

We arrived in New York by the Lincoln Tunnel about midday and booked in at an hotel in Madison Avenue. Being two girls alone in the teeming bustle of New York, we were careful to choose a modest residential hotel rather than one of the soaring chromium caravanserais—at least that is what the hotel seemed in daylight to our inexperienced eyes. Having booked in at the reception desk, we went out to dinner and then saw a play about convicts.

We returned to the hotel later that night. The quietness that had seemed so respectable took on a more menacing aspect. As we scuttled timidly across the hotel lobby, we felt that the night clerk shot us a strange look from under his green eye-shade. We crept into the lift, to find it occupied by three hatchet-faced characters who might have stepped straight out of the pages of Damon Runyon. The bulges in their jackets might have been well-filled wallets but in our present mood of anxiety could just as well have been guns. One of them looked us up and down from behind hooded lids and then muttered to his friends, 'Say, I didn't know they had girls in this dump!'

The lift doors had hardly opened at our floor when Shirley and I leapt out and tore down the corridor to our room, slamming and locking the door behind us. Fortunately the three Public Enemies—for so we thought them to be at this stage—must have considered us too small game and we left the hotel next morning without further incident.

The next day, after hectic Christmas shopping, we went to see Victor Borge in his solo show *Comedy in Music*. We were kept laughing for two and a half hours with the rest of the audience, while he read Shakespeare, punctuated phonetically with noises for commas, stops and colons, and then he mimicked the great composers. After his own idea of a Mozart opera, he acted and played jazz pieces and exaggerated without mercy any popular music sentimentally inclined.

As a child pianist he had been a prodigy, and even then he could not control his great sense of humour. At an important concert in Copenhagen when he was only thirteen the orchestra paused to let him do some solo trills. Suddenly he thought how funny it was that all the important people of the city should have hurried through dinner only to listen to a little boy playing two-finger trills, so he went on trilling and eventually he looked round at the audience and laughed. Later, at the beginning of the war, when he escaped to America he found that he was slowly starving, while trying to earn his living as a concert pianist, so he turned to comedy. Since then he has reduced vast audiences to helpless laughter, and he himself has prospered as he deserved.

We did not risk a second night in New York and left by one of the excellent exit routes from the city. The tunnel took us under the Hudson River in the shortest possible time. Although traffic in New York is terrible, once one leaves the island itself the routes clear the heavy traffic at once.

After spending the night with one of the American show jumping team, Arthur McCashin and his wife, our next stop was Washington. The white houses shone in the brilliant sunshine and I filmed the White House itself, and Thomas Jefferson sitting in his shrine looking down to Cleopatra's Needle and beyond to the splendid Capitol against the skyline. People who live there say that the climate is tropical during the summer, with ticks and poisonous snakes hiding in the woods around Rock Creek. It could not have been more pleasant on that December day.

We got lost on one of the complicated route systems going out of the city in rush hour. Eventually we sorted out our routes and had to go round the circuit again to escape on to the road leading to Virginia, our next stop for some more hunting. We were greeted by kind friends, who gave us horses to hunt with the Orange County, the Piedmont and the Warrington hounds. We rode over the hills, where the great battles of the Civil War had taken place, and were told of the immense casualties suffered by both armies. Our only casualty was one of the riders who fell off in a creek, and must have felt very cold for the rest of the day.

The open country was rather like some of our Cotswold hills, except that the large fields were separated by wire fences. We could jump from field to field over a 'chicken coop' or panel put in the corners of most of the fences. However, this was the only unwired part, whereas in the Cotswolds we can usually jump a wall where we choose.

In Virginia the huntsmen had a hard job when the fox got into the vast forests, and there was the danger of losing hounds or having to stay out half the night to collect them.

One Sunday we heard the chimes of the carillon as we went to church. These bells have been presented to Mr. Fletcher Harper, who was Master of the Orange County foxhounds, from 1920 to 1953. The bells were playing 'D'ye ken John Peel' and followed that with the Doxology.

We left Mr. and Mrs. Oliver Filley, our hosts at Over The Grass Farm, and drove to Wiffle Tree Manor, where Mrs. Windmill had her collection of coaches and harness. We saw sleighs, a hansom cab, a hearse, a surrey with the fringe on top, a one-horse shay and many other horse conveyances that I had already seen in England.

After a good day's hunting the drizzle turned to sleet, and showed us that it was time to go further south. We had wanted to drive to North Carolina along the Blue Ridge Mountains, by the skyline drive looking down to the Shenandoah valley, but as we approached the mountains it started to snow. Obviously it would have

been unwise to risk this slippery snake-like route, so we
kept under the eastern side of the mountains and crossed
vast forests, that hid and sheltered the tobacco clearings.
It was during this drive, through these lonely stretches,
that I had one of my most exciting moments, and nearly
my last.

The narrow strip of concrete road stretched endlessly
ahead like a silver streak. In the distance I saw a truck
approaching before it disappeared behind one of the
many undulations. As we came to a blind crest, travelling at about 80 m.p.h., the truck suddenly appeared
again coming towards us at a speed of at least 70 m.p.h.,
and at the same time being overtaken by another car.
We were too close to stop and the road was too narrow
for all of us. At the last moment the overtaking car
pulled right across me, and shot up the soft bank at the
side of the road. I saw it overturning as I just squeezed
between its tail end, and the truck. I pulled up as quickly
as possible and leapt out. As I ran back down the road,
I could see the car lying on its side, and I had visions of
having to extricate the bodies. At that moment the door
lying uppermost on the car opened like a trap door. A
head emerged, with a battered hat still perched on it.
An old farmer proceeded to follow the hat. After he
had climbed out he leaned down and started to pull at
something in the car. This turned out to be his wife and
by the time I arrived they were both standing safely on
the road. I gasped, 'Are you all right?' and the wife's
only comment was to her husband, 'I guess we dun orter
kep home, stead o' looking for a Christmas tree.'

By this time the three coloured men, who had been in
the truck, had arrived on the scene, and also Shirley who

had been asleep beside me. We all set to trying to get the ancient car on its wheels again, but it was deeply embedded in the sand. There was no garage for miles, in fact this was the first vehicle we had met during our morning's drive. It always seems that one can drive for hours along an isolated road; and then within two hundred yards meet a tractor, a haycart, a car, and a flock of sheep, and all this when coming round a blind corner when travelling rather too fast. However, this time one car had nearly been too much!

Eventually another huge truck pulled up and we all looked hopefully for strong men to emerge. We were disappointed as one tiny coloured fellow clambered out. He saw what was wanted and before we had got back to help him, he put one hand on the overturned car and it rolled back on to its wheels. He must have used magic or else he had a hidden strand of Samson's hair. The old car was not much the worse, in fact it did not even have a crack in the windscreen. After extracting some of the oil, that had tipped into the engine, they started it up and away it chugged, proving the resistant quality of old material.

Driving on to Southern Pines in North Carolina, Shirley kept me awake with a terrible story about her horse-van that had overturned in a fog, when going along that route a year before. In spite of this, we arrived safely, in time to have a pleasant evening talking about hounds and hunting. I learnt that a fox living in this sandy region cannot dig an earth without its collapsing and perhaps suffocating him. Imported red foxes have to have artificial earths made for them, while the grey foxes, natural to this country, live in bushes or trees.

These stories were told in the charming southern dialect of the people living in this district of the Moore County Foxhounds.

One of the members of the hunt was America's leading 'chase jockey, F. Dooley Adams. He came out hunting with us, and his wife who rode Refugio, an old grey horse that had run seventh in our 1950 Grand National.

The next evening we went square-dancing which, like Scottish dancing, or country dancing, is quite easy to learn, only if it is well organized, and your partner knows the steps. I loved the gay cotton skirts on the girls, and the attractive coloured shirts worn by the boys with knotted handkerchiefs instead of collars and ties.

In the morning we were up at the crack of dawn to ride to the meet by 8 a.m., in order to get out hunting before the sun became too hot. The weather played a trick and it was Grandfather Frost who greeted us, at twenty degrees below zero. The sand was frozen in ruts and even the grey tree-climbing foxes must have needed to huddle with the birds for extra warmth that morning. It was obviously time to follow the sun farther south. So at top speed we arrived at Charleston, and for the first time I saw the Spanish moss growing on the trees, giving an eerie effect of the witch's wood in *Snow White*. We went on across the low country between Charleston and Savannah, crossing vast swamps, to the Coo Saw Plantation near Beaufort.

We were unexpected guests, but this did not lessen the welcome given to us by Paul and Eva Fout. Eva had hunted in our country before she had married. Paul, who was an Amateur Steeplechase rider, had broken his back in a bad fall when racing over the solid post and rails in the Maryland Hunt Cup the year before but was now nearly fit again.

The next morning we went out on to the marshes at the crack of dawn to see duck, quail and heron, but the freak cold had left everything frozen. Instead, we returned to the house to look at Paul's Palomino stallion. Paul had just started riding again and without a thought for his back he bravely jumped the horse over some improvised fences. He then saddled a Lippizaner three-year-old that he was only just beginning to handle, and accompanied me on the Palomino as we rode over the marshes. We did not see any alligators, because they prefer to bask in the hot sun, but I saw a Red Cardinal bird and plenty of wood-cock while I listened to stories of the rattlesnakes. These poisonous snakes were taken as a matter of course in plantation life. Luckily the snake makes the rattle noise as it is about to strike, so the sound gives a last-minute warning to kill the snake before he bites.

When we got back we saw some duck on the sea shore. However, when they were shot at, they proved to be hell-divers. Instead of flying they submerged and waited under water until the danger had past. Having had no luck with getting a duck for dinner, we lunched off shrimps and peacons, and grapefruit cooked with port, which made an excellent meal. After lunch, Shirley and I drove on south and very nearly got caught for speeding again. For nearly every state has a speed limit, regardless of how remote one is from human habitations.

We left Georgia with the sunset reflecting its crimson and gold colours in the marshes, and that night we crossed into Florida. We had come South so quickly, that the car radio had to be frequently adjusted as we went out of the range of one station and into the range of a new one. I was intrigued to hear the change of dialect, as we sped from state to state.

When we woke up the next day, there was no frost and we were greeted by the sun. At last we could wear cotton frocks and shed our heavy pullovers.

I enjoyed seeing the old Spanish town of St. Augustine, before we continued along the coast. The style of the houses brought back memories of the week I had spent in Spain nearly three years before. The solid Fort of St. Marko had a notice by the moat, telling of its history when it had been defended against the English.

Driving on down the coast alongside the blue sea we came to a notice inviting us to see 'The Mystery House'. We paid to see its mystery, and discovered that the mystery was the ease with which tourists are fooled. The only thing worth seeing was a model of a mare and foal at the entrance, made out of Spanish moss. Opposite this was the alligator farm, but we made our next stop at the Marine Studios where one could see all the deep-sea fish. Looking through portholes, in an enormous sea-water tank, we watched large turtles floating by, and saw dangerous barracuda, ray-fish, electric eels, sharks, tarpon and dolphins. In other tanks there were brightly coloured little fish, sea horses, and even an octopus. The greatest fun of all was when the keeper lowered a bell into the top of the tank, which he supposedly rang beneath the chopping waves, and at the sound of the dinner bell, out leapt the porpoises ready to be fed. Their graceful jumps were a joy to see, and these huge fish could get enough momentum and accuracy to take

E

food from the keeper's mouth, as he stood on a spring board high above the water.

Driving on through the trees stunted from the sea wind, and the bungalow-type houses, strongly built because of the danger of hurricanes, we came to Daytona. We drove along the beach famous for speed trials because of its hard even surface, but we tourists had a speed limit of 10 miles an hour imposed upon us, because of the danger to bathers. However, this weather, warmer than most English summer days, had proved too cold for the Southerners to risk the fresh air, so we crawled along at our 10 miles an hour on a deserted beach.

The next part of our drive was through the Indian River district, where the most delicious grapefruit and oranges are grown. Instead of stopping for lunch we ate some kum kwats and then bought a bag of smoked shrimps, but alas, the latter evoked a terrible thirst, which did not make itself obvious until we had eaten too many. Most of the shacks sold fruit, and one could buy crates of fresh oranges to send away to one's friends. Several places also sold fruit juice, with a notice saying, 'Ten cents for a glass of fruit juice'. Others more competitive, said, 'Ten cents a glass and a second helping free', but the most daring said, 'Ten cents for all you can drink'. We pulled up smartly at the latter, where the proprietor did not know about our terrible thirst from the smoked shrimps. He looked aghast, as I drank quarts of grapefruit juice, and Shirley consumed nearly a gallon of orange juice. We then made up for this, by buying string bags packed with oranges and grapefruit, which gave us our staple diet for the next few days. Never have I tasted such delicious fruit as this, picked from the trees. It was the difference between the flavour of tomatoes eaten fresh from the plant, firm and warm from the sun, or eating them after they have travelled through shops and waited to be bought, by which time they are tired and uninteresting.

Fort Lauderdale was our destination, and when we arrived I found it like a small Venice, with as many waterways as roads. We discovered a charming apartment on the island near the ocean. It was a bungalow, built around three sides of a sheltered square garden. Each room opened on to the veranda, and we made our double room a base for the next few days.

That night a silvery moon rose in the clear sky, accentuating the shadows of the trees and the lights of the houses. The gardens and trees were floodlit in many colours, mingling with the different greens the beautiful red of the poinsietta flowers. It was like being in Fairyland as we wandered through the palm trees, past a hotel surmounted with Father Christmas driving his reindeer through the warm and scented air. In the town we found a sea-food place for supper. After some delicious Florida crawfish, we returned to our apartment and ate oranges before going to bed.

The great sport of these coasts is deep-sea game fishing, and I longed to try my hand at catching the huge sail fish, tarpon and barracuda. The next day kind friends took us in a boat, round the inland waterways. One visits friends there by tying up the boat at the back door, or driving the car to the front door. We held up traffic as bridges opened to let us pass and swing bridges turned to give us the right of way over motor transport. Boats could still take precedence over cars.

Later that afternoon I was the lone swimmer in a rough sea, despite warnings of 'man o' war' and 'undertow'. The sky was overcast with no sun, but the ocean was warmer than at any time I have bathed off the English coast.

One evening we drove to Miami, and after dining at the lighthouse on the ocean off their speciality of live stone crabs, we went to see a jai-alai game. It was the first time that I had seen this astonishingly fast ball game, that is a speciality of the Basque race. The two players have a basket tied on their right hand, and the ball is caught in the basket to be thrown against the far wall, rebounding for the opponent to catch, and return again against the wall. The speed of the ball is almost faster than the eye can see, and it rebounds with a tremendous force. I put my money on Carlitos, a tough little Spaniard from the Basque country, aged about sixteen. These lads play six times a week, sometimes three times a night, and with a ten-week stretch. The strain is tremendous, and like bull fighters, they earn their money at an early age, and then have to retire. While we were watching this enthralling game, Shirley discovered that she had lost her car keys. She nipped off and found a locksmith, who made a duplicate set within an hour, and by the time the game was over, the car was again in working order.

Shirley had to be home for Christmas, so the car was left in Florida, after it had carried us faithfully for 3,000 miles. We caught a plane for Tampa on the western side of Florida, where a T.C.A. plane took us back to Toronto. On the long and noisy flight back North we saw little of the territory that we had so recently driven through, but in the evening from the west side of the

plane, I watched the sun setting behind the Blue Ridge
Mountains, now topped with snow. The sky turned
from golden to red before the darkness absorbed all shades
of colour.

After another change of plane, we arrived in the snow
at Ottawa, just as Christmas Eve was dawning. That
night we went to Midnight Mass, before a quiet Christmas
Day at home, spent eating, and opening presents from
under the tree. Later in the evening some friends came
in and two of the boys played the violin and accordion
with expert ease. We had games of bingo, ping-pong
and snooker, and in between whiles I told stories and was
horrified later to find that they had been tape-recorded.

II

GRASS COUNTRY

While we were working off our Christmas dinner, dancing Virginian reels, the telephone rang and the call was for
me. It was my cousin Ralph Beermann, from Nebraska,
ringing to say that he would meet me in Chicago, if I could
get there, in two days' time. I had no special plans about
getting home, so I accepted the invitation with alacrity.
After a farewell party, I left the hospitality of the Thomases
and caught a plane at 5 a.m. in a snow storm. Flying
from Toronto to Chicago, we arrived out of a bank of
cloud, over the great lake, to see the waterfront and the
skyscrapers of the city, shining in the clear sunlight. I
met Ralph immediately, as he had followed our plane in
on to the landing strip with his little Piper Pacer. As we

transferred my cases which barely fitted in the back seat, I felt a bit dubious about its size, but bravely strapped myself in. My confidence was restored, as Ralph handled the plane with as much ease as I can ride a horse.

I must admit that my heart was in my mouth as we did one or two quick and steep turns, in order to see the stock yards more clearly. I would not have minded turning a polo pony in this way, but with a plane the feeling was very different!

We arrived in Rockford, Illinois, to meet more friends and relations, and the Press. I was fairly tired after the all-night farewell party and then a journey involving three changes of plane, but I have a note in my 'greedy book' that I was strengthened by lunching at the May-flower, off shrimps and a 'grasshopper'. I seem to recall that the 'grasshopper' was liquid refreshment, made of brandy, crème de menthe and ice-cream, or whipped cream. It is fabulous the amount of recipes one can collect in America, not only for foods but for delicious liquid concoctions.

New Year's Eve was spent listening to midnight broadcasts from Times Square, New York, Chicago, Denver and San Francisco, each with a different hour according to their position further west.

Ralph had to fly back to Nebraska on business while we went by bus to Davenport in Iowa. I was glad that I did not miss the drive along Rock River to Dixon, seeing Blackhawke monument, as a memory to the Indians that lived in that valley not so long ago.

I discovered more relations in Davenport, who took me to the birthplace of Buffalo Bill Cody, at Le Claire on the banks of the Mississippi River.

Ralph then arrived to pick me up in the Pacer, so that I could fly back with him to Sioux City. However, we were diverted en route, by the lure of new Bonanza planes at Cedar Rapids. We landed and had some trial trips in these fast little aircraft. While we were checking the controls before take-off, another Bonanza flew in to land and only just unfolded its wheels as it touched the air-strip. The instructor with us swore, and said, 'That son of a gun is too sure of himself to bother with routine, he's getting careless with his flying and one of these days he'll find it's too late to check.'

After the superior and modern Bonanza, the Pacer must have felt her propeller put out of joint, but she carried us back, over the Missouri valley and the Beermann farms and into Sioux City.

We got back just in time to hear General Romulo, a Philipino, talk on the importance of Asia in world affairs. He had been General McArthur's aide and then held the important post of Speaker in the U.N.O. It was unexpected luck that I should have heard him give this most interesting talk.

The next day, I was introduced to Ralph's brother, Melvin, who had a Palomino horse. Melvin gave me my first lesson in spinning a lariat, and Tex the stallion was patient when I got the rope tangled round the wrong object. In the evening I was taken with the family to watch a wrestling match. It started with two girls, who were great actors but not a pretty spectacle. Then the men came on but both were counted out on their third fall. However, we did see one good championship match, which I was told was the real thing, with the wrestlers throwing each other with a sleeper-hold or a full nelson, and once being floored by three successive 'double-foot flying kicks'. Even then it is not a sport that I like, and I was more interested by the faces of the fanatics in the audience than the actual fighting itself.

The following day I went to the Auditorium in Sioux City for my initiation into the exciting game of basket-ball. I was lucky enough to see a championship game, with the Harlem Globe Trotters, the coloured team, against the House of David, with their bearded players. It was a superb game, and the control over the ball and the clowning of the experts was a display of artistry only found among top class players in any sport. One of the Globe Trotters had only one arm, but he controlled the ball as easily as the rest of the team.

We arrive after the evening's entertainment had begun and had a tussle to find a seat and a programme. During the interval it was announced that Sam Wheeler, the leading player of the Globe Trotters, would draw the lucky programme number for a radio clock. I had never won a prize in any raffle either at school or at a church fête. I could not believe it when Sam read out the number of my programme, from among the thousands there. Figure by figure and each one tallied 6, 7, 8, 5, 3, 7. I was speechless and Ralph looked over my shoulder to see why I was gaping. In the silence the number was repeated, Ralph saw my programme and gave a great Indian war whoop. He then led me down over tiers of crowded seats to collect my prize! The bitter rider to this happy story was the fact that in America both the voltage and the clock cycles are quite different from England, making this unique radio set suitable only for use in America!

By this time I had been introduced to all the Beermann family, which was a fair test of memory. There were many brothers and sisters, all of whom were married and several of them already had large families. All were united in the same grass-drying business, with each person taking a different branch according to his knowledge and suitability. This method was extremely successful and provided an entirely family concern working at maximum efficiency and production. Ralph was the salesman and dealt with the publicity and public relations side. Hence the necessity for an aeroplane to cover the vast distances between likely clients all over the States. He had learnt to fly after the war when he came out of the Army. The Piper Pacer was doing its job very well for the firm, but Ralph was longing for the faster and more up to date Bonanza plane with a far greater range.

I quickly understood this idea, and with extreme tact I extolled the superior flying virtues of the Bonanza to the other brothers. The side of the family concerned with the agriculture were more cautious about spending a great sum of dollars on a plane that could only depreciate in value and not even help with the actual grass production.

I was hoping to go to Texas before the end of the month, a journey of more than 1,500 miles, easily covered by a Bonanza but impracticable by other means of transport in the short time I had. My interest was great in the meeting of the brothers to discuss whether it would pay the firm to buy a Bonanza for Ralph to fly faster and further afield.

While these discussions were in progress no grass had a chance to dry under *my* feet. I was taken to Lincoln, the state capital of Nebraska, and met the Governor in his new and impressive building. Nebraska was proud to be one of the few States that had already paid for its capitol building. This was pointed out as a great achievement, and I was shown the expensively decorated interior, ranging from imported marble to buffalo carvings. In the Governor's room one of the heavy tapestries was lifted up to show a secret elevator, in case of emergency and a quick get away!

That day, Marjorie Beermann had lent me her fur coat to guard against the cold. I found that my hair was full of electricity all the time that I was in America, but with the fur coat on I was thoroughly charged! The coat seemed to generate electricity and the dry cold made a perfect medium. Every time I was introduced to someone and shook hands, sparks flew between us and we would get an an electric shock. It was reminiscent of the time my brother made me hold a home-made electric shocking machine in the common room of his prep school, while his young friends tried various voltages of current through 'Smythe's sister' to find out when she would flinch.

I began to get quite cautious about shaking hands, especially as I would be greeted by uninhibited remarks like, 'I feel you're having a sparking good time', or 'America's put you in shocking form', or even, 'It sure gave me a shock to meet this bright young spark.'

At the television station in Lincoln I had been given an introduction to the manager of Denver Stock Show and Rodeo. Ralph's younger brother Lowell and his wife were driving to Colorado for the show and kindly asked me to come with them. I arrived in the evening at their house in time for a very good dinner of oyster stew. After an hour or two's sleep we got up at 3 a.m. and started our journey well before dawn. We stopped for breakfast when it was getting light, but I could not face waffles at that time of the morning! On across the plains where I saw coyotes slinking off in the distance, and up and down the undulations and rolling land driving at full speed. Towards evening, the Rocky Mountains appeared over the horizon and then filled the background as we came closer to Denver. We drove into the city as it was getting dusk, having covered six hundred and twenty miles that day.

I was fascinated by the whole atmosphere of the city during Rodeo time, when the streets are filled with genuine cowboys and stockmen with their families, taking the chance of shopping and window gazing at the town luxuries. I felt out of place in my conventional clothes, and so I changed into blue jeans, a check shirt with a knotted handkerchief round my neck and some soft leather cowboy boots. Dressed comfortably like this, I joined the crowd at the show looking at all the various stock. The most numerous and valuable stock were the exhibition of beef cattle, Aberdeen Angus and Herefords being the most popular breeds.

I was shown two enormous Holsteins standing $19\frac{1}{2}$ hands high and supposedly the two largest steers in the world. The stockmen and hard-faced dealers standing around had been trying to guess the weight of these steers and they asked me for my opinion. We had weighed our horses before flying them to America and I thought that each of the steers looked about as heavy as Prince Hal and Tosca's combined weights. When I had converted hundredweights into pounds, the tough cattlemen were astounded that my guess was nearer the correct weight than any of theirs. I was one pound out on the lighter steer and nine pounds out on the heavier. Although these were the highest steers I have seen, there were three Santa Gertrudis six-year-olds on the King Ranch in Texas that also weighed over 2,600 lb. a piece.

During the show the auctioneers were busy with the stock sales and I listened to their singing chant, 'I have five, five, five, there's a five, and a half, now it's five and a half, give me six, give me six,' and so on until each animal changed hands at different prices but to the accompaniment of the same chant and rhythm of the auctioneer's voice.

Most of my time was spent at the Rodeo, which I found by following the 'This-a-way' signs. I watched the opening of the show, with all the exhibitors in the ring together on their best parade horses, covered with gay trappings and decorated hand-worked western saddlery. Then the cowboys tightened their belts, fastened their leather chaps and pulled down their hats more securely before concentrating on the tough game of riding bare back broncos or Brahma bulls. There was also the art of calf roping and steer wrestling and the prettiest sight of all—the cutting horse contest. This event calls for a most intelligent horse, who does the best part of the work itself, separating the calves and anticipating their dodges, with the minimum assistance from its rider. In fact marks are deducted by the judges if they see the horse being guided by its rider.

In this atmosphere of the wild west, I met 'America's most beloved cowboy,' Tex Ritter, with his friend 'Happy', who was always in trouble. We had a long chat after he had finished his show in the Skyline

Room at the Top of the Park, one of the highest buildings in Denver. Although the city is snugly at the foot of the Rocky Mountains, the approach across the plains is a gradual ascent. I was astonished to see an ordinary skyscraper called the 'Mile High', only to find that this was the authentic altitude above sea level.

By then Ralph had caught up with us in the Pacer, since the possibility of a Bonanza was still in the discussion stage. So Ralph flew to Denver and borrowed a car to take me on a quick two-day trip in Colorado.

We drove south towards Colorado Springs, making a detour to see the Garden of the Gods. On the rough approaches we got a flat tyre, and it was twilight by the time we reached the magnificent gateway of huge slabs of rock, jutting into the sky. The vast and natural rock formations and the huge mushroom of balanced rock, silhouetted against the evening sky, gave the simple feeling of the power of God, a humbling effect after being surrounded by man-made skyscrapers. Apart from crowds and in the stillness of the dusk one could think more clearly than in the noisy whirl of city life.

It was snowing the next day but we braved the skiddy roads to the Royal Gorge, where I stood on the highest suspension bridge in the world and looked down 1,200 feet to the Arkansas River below. A blizzard was blowing and the wind and snow whistled up the gorge making the bridge swing as we drove across. We went on to the knife-edge ridge topped with a narrow road aptly called the 'sky line drive'. If one dared to take one's eyes off the icy track, there was Canyon City and the famous penitentiary in the distance.

As we drove farther into the Rocky Mountains and

climbed higher, the weather cleared and there was no trace of snow. This was just as well, as we were driving through lonely remote valleys, with only a few isolated ranches, far from any town. The colours of the mountains became every shade of purple and mauve, unbelievable unless one has seen them in this light.

Miles from anywhere we came to a little town called Guffey with a population of about fifty people. There were one or two small mines there, but not enough to attract outsiders. The dear old couple at the Post Office gave me pieces of lead, silver, gold, copper and nickel from the mines. They were thrilled to talk to people from the outside world, and told us of their troubles a year or two before when everything they possessed had been burnt when their house caught fire. With hard work, faith and no money, they had rebuilt the Post Office and had settled down in their contented life, happier than most people who are surrounded with luxuries.

In the dark we drove on to the ghost town of Cripple Creek. Fifty-odd years ago the valuable mines had made this a thriving city of about 65,000 people. The price of gold had dropped and the cost of labour increased when people left the city in the 1920's until now there are only a few hundred of the older generation living there. It was weird driving through deserted streets of empty houses, and past the disused Grand Opera House. On the outskirts of the city, the tipheaps and rusting machinery looked grotesque in the moonlight.

We had stopped for a few minutes at the inn, which was as empty as the town. Apart from the general feeling of depression, the innkeeper was suffering from a broken arm, which did not help him to paint a brighter picture of his home town.

While we were climbing the 10,000-foot pass through Divide to Colorado Springs, a cougar mountain lion retreated from our headlights until only his fiery eyes glowed in the darkness as he crouched in fury at our intrusion.

Leaving Pike's Peak and the memorial to Will Rogers standing out on the mountain side, we drove back to Denver Airport. The Pacer was waiting to fly us faithfully back over the stretches of wheat land looking flat from above, but marked by contour ploughing and deep-cut creeks. We landed at Grand Island to look wistfully at another Bonanza, and then flew on in the dark to Sioux City. On the way we nearly got cut in two by an Air Force jet fighter, yet another argument for the superior radio apparatus and flying lights on the Bonanza.

I could not leave Sioux City before seeing the White Horse Mounted Patrol. These horses were owned privately but trained together to do circus tricks as well as parade with their owners at various displays through the country. Their trainer, Bob Taylor, played the organ extremely well, which is a proof that music and understanding of horses often go together. One of the horses actually sat up and begged like a dog, and in this position conducted an orchestra of horses!

A final meeting of the brothers was held one morning while I was looking round the grass-drying plant. At lunch, when one of the company was telling me my fate by the stars, Ralph came in with a broad grin, that could not hide the fact that the Bonanza was at last a reality. No time was wasted. We rushed to the airport and had a trial trip in the new aircraft before it got dark, in fact we used the powerful landing lights on our return, a change from groping down and feeling for the runway in the Pacer.

We were at the airport checking for our take-off into the cold morning at 8 a.m. the next day. I had said good-bye to the many kind friends around Sioux City and now we were on our way to Southern Texas. We flew in the clear air at about 8,000 feet over Omaha and Lincoln. The Bonanza made little of the distance, although it had taken us a long morning's drive when I had visited Lincoln by car.

We were experimenting with the various new gadgets on the plane, and the good radio with V.H.F. stations. I was told about the A.D.F. (automatic direction finder) and Omnigator, and I was trying to be intelligent about Zee markers, Fan markers and the cone of silence over the range stations, when a weather report came through. There was a cold front ahead and we were advised to drop to 1,000 feet.

We saw the masses of cloud ahead and still had another 1,000 feet to come down by the time we were in the swirl of cold and foggy mist. The warm temperature in the sunlight higher up dropped when we came lower. As we flew through the cloud, ice began forming on the wings, and the plane became heavier. The fog and icing conditions forced us to fly below the ceiling of cloud. Low flying in a fast plane is no joke if one does not know the lie of the land or the whereabouts of high masts or hills. The visibility got worse and Ralph decided to land at St. Joseph to wait for the ceiling of cloud to lift. We went to the control tower to survey the cold airfield and find out if there was any hope of better weather.

There seemed no chance of its clearing, so we decided to make for a more civilized place. In the air again, we flew in silence watching for icing on the wings and Ralph studied the maps to find the best route for Kansas City. We had the undercarriage down to slow the plane up at the low altitude and with such limited visibility. Meantime Ralph mentioned wistfully how much safer and more manoeuvrable was the Piper Pacer in bad flying conditions.

We made the airfield that lies by the river down below Kansas City. Luckily we had avoided the skyscrapers towering up into the foggy clouds, but as we came in on the misty landing strip, we saw the wreck of an aircraft on the river bank.

For two more days there was no more flying in or out of the airport, but we were comfortably staying with my friends the Durands. Carol Durand, who has a small son, had been in the U.S.A. jumping team and I knew her from the shows in America and at home. She and her husband Dana, met us at the airport and took us into town for a zombie-rum, to warm us up and restore our confidence! Once we were again on 'terra firma', we realized more than ever that our day's flying had not been exactly 'a piece of cake'.

During the two days we saw many of the thoroughbred horses around Kansas City, one of which, Lawrin had won the 1939 Kentucky Derby. While I was getting up to date with the local horse population, Ralph managed to do some business to justify this half-way stopping place.

Before we left I had the usual Press interview, as somehow the American Press are very much on the alert and always knew more about my plans than I did myself!

Once I was caught I enjoyed the interviews, as the people were genuinely interested in our lives over here, and not so very many ordinary English people get the chance to journey through the Middle West.

As soon as the weather was clear, we were in the air heading for Texas. We passed over Independence, Kansas, Tulsa in Oklahoma and the Canadian River to Ardmore, the birthplace of Will Rogers. At last we came to Red River and into Texas, landing at Fort Worth to refuel.

We also refuelled ourselves with a quick lunch before flying on to the Texas State Capital at Austin. With the independence of our own plane, we could sightsee from the air, flying round the capitol and university before heading east of San Antonio and on south over the prairie to Alice.

It began to get more misty as we met the cold front that had now moved into the warmer South, dissolving into moist cloud. We came down lower and followed the pipe-lines across endless stretches of scrubby mesquite and cactus, spotted across the plain. Occasionally we came over an oil well, surrounded by a cluster of huts, but then again for miles there would be no sign of life except for scattered groups of grazing cattle.

I began to think how dull the prairie must be, flat and all exactly the same. Little did I know then of the clear colours, the sunrise and sunset, the peace and the fascination of the life there.

I wondered if Ralph had any idea where we were in this vast State. He was checking the weather report from Alice, and apparently from the look on his face it was none too clear there. He turned to me and said, 'Maybe we'd better head for Laredo and wait for this cloud to lift.' I was in full agreement for, apart from the unnecessary risk one takes when flying a small plane in bad visibility, I was longing to see Mexico. Laredo is right on the border and I was sure that once we reached there, I could get across the Rio Grande and set foot in Mexico, visa or no visa.

The next moment Ralph decided to keep on his course for a few minutes more, to see if we were in striking distance of the King Ranch. I had no faith in our positioning, when out of the mist below us loomed a village of tiny white houses. There was a creek leading past a large yard surrounded by buildings, and an oblong racecourse nearby. Over beyond the racecourse was a palatial and shining white house, built in a rectangle around a courtyard, dominated on one side by a tower.

The enormous field beyond had the grass mown in landing strips, so that one could come in from any direction.

We circled low, and I felt thrilled to see the centre of this great ranch, and our destination below us. There were two cars at the front door with people standing around them. I was sure they would look up and wave or stare, as though we were men from Mars, or explorers from the Antarctic, but they noticed our presence as little as we trouble about the newest jets breaking the sound barrier over our Cotswold hills.

Having created no sensation at the ranch house, we set about landing. The undercarriage was lowered and everything checked, but as we came in, we saw horses were grazing on our landing strip. We roared over their heads, to try and frighten them away, but they were as unimpressed as the people at the ranch house, and never moved. After circling a few more times, Ralph found just enough room to squeeze down between two chestnuts, a dun and a bay. As we landed the bay mare turned her tail towards us in disgust. We taxied to the wire fence and climbed out of the plane having covered 800 miles during the previous six hours.

III

THE HEART OF TEXAS

A car arrived at the fence, and a Mexican got out to say that he would take us to the ranch house. I was relieved to find that we had been noticed and we were quickly driven to the house, which was even larger than I had first imagined from the air.

We found that my hosts, the Klebergs, would not be back from another division of the ranch until the next day, but we were made most welcome and dined off the best Santa Gertrudis beef. The history of this breed is most interesting.

The cattle men were searching for an animal which would thrive in heat and resist disease, in spite of ticks and flies. The cattle they had to work with were Herefords and Durhams (Shorthorns) which came from the native Longhorns of Spanish origin. These cows were put to good beef bulls, bought at the American shows. Many of the bulls were English bred and imported for their excellent beef qualities. Then a new experiment was made with the Brahma (Zebu) cattle, with good milking qualities and extremely resistant to heat, diseases and pests.

Bob Kleberg as a young man was allowed to experiment from certain breeds. From a cross of three-eighths Brahma cattle, the humped Indian breed that puts on only little meat, and five-eighths Shorthorn, with the meat producing qualities without the stamina to withstand drought and parasites, a bunch of calves was produced.

From these calves, one young bull called Monkey had all the necessary qualities that they required. He thrived on poor grazing and put on quality meat, without being unduly worried by drought or parasites. What was more, he was a freak of breeding in that without fail he transmitted his qualities to his offspring. Monkey was the foundation of the breed of Santa Gertrudis, named after the Spanish land grant that gave its name to the creek on which the main ranch house is built. The calves of this line could put on three pounds of weight a day with only the poor prairie grazing, and at the same time become good quality beef.

I found myself right amongst these red cattle. They were the centre of all business and prosperity. It was through them that the racehorses could prosper in luxurious conditions, and be bred according to scientific experiment with various lines of blood, rather than by the nearest economic possibility.

The next morning I was up early to see the two-year-olds working out on the racecourse. The young stock here in the warmth of the south were much more forward than the same aged yearlings and two-year-olds that I had seen in Kentucky, farther north. They worked well in their gallops and were excellently cared for by Mexican lads, who treated their charges with more care than children. This is no empty saying, because the Latin races do put their children before anything else.

After seeing the thoroughbred horses, I was shown the separate establishments with the quarter horses. These were the basic blood for the cow ponies, used for working the cattle. A quarter horse originally got its name from being able to gallop a quarter of a mile faster than a thoroughbred. They were smaller but more strongly built, so that they could jump off the mark and be galloping flat out in a moment. Likewise they could stop and turn in a flash if necessary, which is ideal for their work with cattle. I loved their intelligent little heads and when I rode some of these quarter horses during the round-up, I found that they could think far more quickly than I could. They knew the work from generations of breeding for this job, and they could tell which way the cattle were going to turn and the best way to cut them away from the herd.

I saw many horses, and secretly thought what a brilliant international jumper one could produce, by crossing the intelligent and strong little quarter horse with a larger quality thoroughbred. I found then that there were other small herds of different breeds of cattle on the ranch, kept for interest and used as well for experimental breeding. There were the hump-backed, dun coloured Brahmas, the Indian cattle. These ugly and gaunt looking beasts I had seen in the bucking contests at the Rodeo. Not only could they twist athletically as they gave impossible bucks, but they would turn on their would-be rider as soon as he fell off.

I kept one foot on the running board of the van when we went to look at the huge Afrikander cattle. The

[74]

wide span of horn was frightening enough, but I had also been warned that they were not exactly domestic animals! To restore my nerve I was shown some English Park cattle. These pretty white cattle with darker markings I did know about, as one or two herds are preserved in England. I was surprised to meet them in Texas and it was explained to me that some had been shipped over at the beginning of the war for an exhibition. In spite of their domestic-sounding name, they were actually the wildest and the meanest of all the cattle. Their origin dated back to the forebears of the Spanish fighting bulls found in the Pyrenees.

The last lot of cattle we had to rout out of the drinking hole, and then when they came charging up through the bush, we ran for the car! They were the Texas Long-horns, the original wild cattle found roaming the prairie when Captain King first saw this land while riding through Corpus Christi on business trips from Browns-ville to Austen. Eventually he bought great tracts of this 'no-man's-land' and bandit country and he started ranching there in the middle of the last century.

The cattle were not much good for beef, before they were crossed with our good beef breeds. Then the problem was to try to find cattle that were tough enough to survive on the prairie. Seeing these 'pure' Longhorns made me think that, like Samson's hair, all their strength must be in their horns, which grew endlessly out each side, with turned up points just to impress one with the full span.

It was damp and foggy on the first morning that I was taken to help in the round-up. We drove across miles of prairie with the mesquite trees looking like eerie ghosts in the mist. Luckily the car had puncture-proof tyres, because we passed through cactus plants, prickily pear and over broken branches of mesquite. Often we had to force a way through the undergrowth. This southern division of the ranch had once been a lawless part of its own, until it came within the State of Texas when the Americans claimed the Rio Grande as their border line, instead of the smaller Nueces river farther north near Corpus Christi. It had been very difficult to get the ownership of the land established, and the founders of the ranch had sometimes to pay taxes to both the Mexicans and Americans, as well as actually buying the land from its various occupants and the Spanish family who had the original land grant. So the title was eventually cleared by buying from two sources.

The ranch was spread over about a million acres and although I rarely saw a fence, I was told that the fences on the ranch covered eighteen thousand miles.

Eventually we arrived at the yards where later some of the cattle would be sorted and loaded into trucks, to be transported to the markets, or just taken to the other parts of the ranch.

From there it was only a mile or two away to the place where the cattle are rounded up and sorted. There are only a few places on the ranch where this is possible, as the soil will blow away after cattle have trampled it for a day or more, unless it has a certain substance in the sub-soil. When a suitable area of this soil is found, the round-up is always held in this place.

I learnt more about cattle in that day's work than I had ever taught myself through clubs and studying agricultural books.

It was dark before the 'Running W' had been branded on the last calf. The syringes were put away after innoculating against disease, the irons used for earmarking and branding were taken out of the fire and cooled off, and the fires scattered and stamped out.

We then rode back having seen a vivid red sunset through the dust raised by the milling herd. Now the moon lay on its back in the evening sky with its points idly kicking upwards. It was attended by large clear stars and against the glow of the western sky were silhouettes of the deer feeding on the horizon. The air was full of the noises of crickets in the grass and the occasional sound of frightened wild turkeys as they scuttled out of our way. We dined on one of the turkeys when we arrived back at the charming one-storey ranch house. Later that night the slatted door of my bedroom, opening on to the veranda, let in the whispering prairie sounds that lulled me to sleep.

After the rush of life in many parts of America I loved the outlook of all the people on the ranch. The cowboys and Mexicans had a great sense of humour and although the work was hard, it seemed to be much more fun than the terrible battle for money that was the only aim in life for many business people.

April Fool's day meant nothing to these straight-faced cattlemen. In fact there was sure to be a leg pull in nearly everything they said. For instance, the horses used for cutting out, or separating of cattle, were often quicker in following the dodges of the calves than the rider. If a rider had fallen off, it could be very dangerous with a great herd of a hundred cattle churning up the dust, the anxious cows searching for their calves, and the dangerous bulls upset by the round-up and looking for trouble.

The other cowboys would always rescue someone in real difficulties, but if they spotted a cowboy caught napping and almost unseated when his horse stopped too quickly, there would be shouts of, 'That's no cutting horse, he's a quitting horse!'

Before I left, I had seen the great machines for clearing the mesquite trees and undergrowth from the prairie. These two monsters cleared four acres an hour each, laying everything low that came in their path. The broken branches and roots were then left to rot for four years, while the wire grass and vegetation began to grow under the dead brush. If the wood had been collected and burnt, leaving the prairie clear, the wind would have blown all the soil away. By leaving the broken brush, the grass established itself by the time the branches had rotted and crumbled, so providing good grazing for the cattle.

From the mesquite and prickly pear of the inland parts of the ranch, the scenery changed to low green forests and *motts* of live oak towards the coast. Then from the top of the sand hills I saw the Laguna Madre, calm and lovely, sheltered from the open sea by a distant low reef. Near the sea were fresh-water lakes, covered with duck. Farther north on the fertile land near Corpus Christi we saw thousands of geese feeding in the alfalfa fields.

Ralph and Marjorie telephoned one night from New Orleans. They had taken the Bonanza there for a convention. I believe it was a meeting of the people interested in fertilizers. They hoped that I could join them in this old French town, famous for the birth of the blues! I longed to go there to see the city and to hear some of the jazz being played in its original surroundings. Unfortunately New Orleans was about as far from the King Ranch as Vienna is from London, and so there was not much chance of my getting there.

Whilst on the subject of great distances in America, I knew of two people who lived very comfortably near New Orleans. They had a lovely and spacious house, built in the prosperous plantation days, and they were well looked after by faithful coloured servants. One day the wife put through a long distance telephone call to her husband, who had to go to Washington on political business. Later that day the call still had not come through. In the evening the coloured 'Mammy' mentioned to her, 'Say M'am, we've had a crazy caller all day, each time I lifts that lil' ol' telephone he says "Long distance to Washington," so I says "Sure is, man" and I jus' puts it down again.'

People who have not travelled around America, especially those who have been short of dollars and transport, have no idea of the vast proportions of the country. I had reached Texas by the kindness of friends, but I still had no money or a way of getting home. A telegram arrived while I was working on the round-up, seventy-five miles from the nearest town. A young Mexican rode up to me and said someone had asked him if he could deliver the telegram to whoever it was on the envelope. I opened it, surprised that anyone could have tracked me down and it read 'LONDON DEMANDS YOUR IMMEDIATE RETURN. . . .'

I had my return ticket to London from New York, but the distance from New York to Texas is just as far.

I finished the day's work and hoped that somehow the problem of getting right across America to New York would solve itself. Somehow luck was on my side and helped by the great kindness of all the Americans that I met, I was in New York within a week.

It happened that a plane had flown someone to the King Ranch from Houston, and I got a lift back in the plane to this wealthy city and hub of the oil world. It was slightly farther east around the Gulf of Mexico, and so a little nearer New York for me. I contacted friends there, whom I had met during the Madison Square Show, and went to stay with them for a couple of days.

I still did not know how to make the next two thousand miles, but there was a lot to see in Houston, the sun was warm and I was sure that things would be all right.

We went to the rodeo that evening, which since I had seen it in Denver, had toured down south calling at Fort Worth on the way, before I caught up with it again at Houston. The Brahma bull riding was terrific and the contest was won by Buck Rutherford, who certainly knew how to sit those wicked, twisting masses of bucking hump-backed bull. I felt that now I was more of a connoisseur of the rodeo events, having actually worked with cattle on the King Ranch! I also met the Mexicans, Cisco and Pancho, known as the Cisco Kids, who are television stars and idols of all the children. Then there was the clown George Mills who diverted the wild bulls, and although he was clowning when he made the bulls chase him, usually it was to give a cowboy time to escape after a fall in the bareback bull riding contest.

We drove around the Shamrock Hotel on the way back, and I was dazed by this fabulous place. Some of the private houses around Houston were fabulous too. They ranged from Montecello to Mount Vernon, and from a dignified Georgian style to modern types, which meant any concoction that the architect could make really different and unlike any other previously known type of habitation.

When we got back, we soon forgot this trend of modern ideas when we played records of *flamenco* singing accompanied by the stirring playing of the guitars. This took our thoughts back to the gipsies who live in the caves near Granada, and never worry themselves about oil wells, more exotic houses, or bigger and better cars. So we finished the evening with the Spanish toast, 'Health, wealth and love, and time to enjoy them all.'

On the second evening we went to a cocktail party and I was introduced to the director of an oil company. We talked of Texas, and then America, with the conversation turning to Europe and then England. I mentioned that I was going back home and I was on my way to New York, and the director asked me why I did not fly to New York with him in his plane the next morning. Would a start of 7 a.m. be too early for me? It certainly was not too early for me, so by the next evening I had seen the swamps around the Mississippi in Lousiana and flown on over Alabama. In Georgia, I thought of Scarlett O'Hara in *Gone with the Wind* as we flew around Atlanta. From the comfort of the twin-engined Lockhead Loadstar, I was able to look down on Washington and then see the skyscrapers of Manhattan soaring up as we came nearer. We circled over La Guardia Airfield, and the spears of Wall Street in the distance became shrouded in the evening mist and then disappeared behind the nearer buildings as we came in to land.

I thanked my friends, feeling how inadequate anything I could say could repay their kindness. When I said good-bye, I found I was standing surrounded by my collection of a suitcase, a bag, a pair of leather chaps, cowboy boots, a horsehair rope for exercising Tosca at home, a rawhide headcollar for Prince Hal and a book, *Life on the King Ranch*. I pulled myself together, realizing that the sunny South was now seven hours flying time behind me. I could not dream in New York and so I collected my things and joined in the endless rush for cabs, for telephones, for the City. Where was I going? I did not know. Then I remembered—to London.

I could not find my return ticket, in fact I could not remember ever having had it when I came over with the horses three months before. Anyway there was no freighter plane for five days so I would just have to wait.

Eventually I found myself in a friend's house with five days in which to see New York. In spite of the sleet and snow the next day, which gave me the idea to see the wonderful film of *The Conquest of Everest*, the time sped by. I had the luck to see the Queen Mary steaming out of the Hudson River, while I was viewing New York from the top of the Empire State Building. However I got home before her, after another night in New York when Mr. and Mrs. Alfred Vanderbilt took me to see the ballet. I was thrilled and impressed with the New York ballet and slightly startled at the modern dancing with Maria Tallchief in *The Filling Station*.

The next day I was back in London and met our own ballet dancer Violetta Elvin in Peter Duncan's programme of *In Town To-night*.

The several thousand miles I had travelled through

America by car and plane, the vivid and varied impressions I had received of this great and uninhibited country, had driven from my mind the real reason for my trip to the States. Without wishing to appear falsely modest, I had genuinely half-forgotten the fact that the horses and I had achieved some show-jumping successes. I was brought back to reality with a bump within minutes of landing at London Airport.

Apart from the Press and the B.B.C. a number of publishers approached me demanding that I should write a book about my experiences. I was reluctant to agree, partly because I felt my life was full enough already without adding writing to my other tasks and partly because of that wish to avoid 'showing off' which seems to be ingrained in most English people. Although I had written three unfinished books before I was twelve, I managed to keep clear of literary entanglements for a week or two but then made the cardinal error of listening to a particularly persuasive literary agent and found myself at a lunch table with my prospective publishers. Even so, I might have wriggled off the hook until a chance remark showed that my host shared my admiration for *flamenco* music. The conversation brisked up, the ice was broken and soon I found myself meekly signing a contract, condemning myself, or so it seems at times, to an unending treadmill.

As a strictly amateur writer, I have to confess that publishers' deadlines are not quite as awesome as they would be to my more professional colleagues. It says much for their kindness and restraint that my publishers and I are still firm friends. Strangely enough, that same literary agent and I are still on speaking terms, but as he is eyeing me beadily while I write these lines (which incidentally should have been delivered nearly a month ago) I had better say no more. As I point out to him frequently, it is not so easy to write with one hand when the other is being twisted behind one's back!

FIRST CONVERSATION PIECE

It was after lunch on Sunday when Prince Hal and Tosca came to the stable door to have a chat before their Siesta, as Hal has called it since visiting Spain.

HAL: Well, we have had a busy week, and you've jumped quite well.

TOSCA: I must say you have not been so bad your-self . . . at times.

HAL: (*indignantly*) What do you mean 'at times'?

TOSCA: Oh, you chaps are so careless and don't keep your mind on the job. I saw you making advances to Finesta the other day.

HAL: (*anxiously*) It was only because I thought it was you, my dear.

TOSCA: I can't see anything in her favour, except that she is grey.

HAL: You conceited thing!

TOSCA: Well I do think I was super at those parallel bars.

HAL: Why?

TOSCA: Well, didn't you see my jockey give me that frightful jab, and then three terrible kicks in the wind, enough to give any respectable mare hiccups?

HAL: Go on with you, you were scampering along and would have met it all wrong. Then you'd have fallen over your nose, and trodden all over her and the poles.

TOSCA: Don't bring up that subject again. What

happened that unlucky time just happened. Anyway it's a closed incident. I must say it was jolly funny at the Royal Show when she fell off in that oxer and peeped at me over the top of the hedge. I would have laughed if I hadn't known that I would be scolded for stopping. I suppose you meet every fence perfectly, as that Italian chap, Mr. Caprilli, used to say.

HAL: Well, I wouldn't like to say that, but I'd rather have a go at the fence from miles out, only she messes about till about two strides away. Slow thinking, that's what I say.

TOSCA: Just like a man, always wants his own way and blames someone else if he can't get it. Anyway, you can't be so perfect, I saw you have a gate down last week.

HAL: It wasn't my fault, didn't you hear Pat say that she'd lost her stride just in front of the gate, only by the time the competition was through it was too late to go back and look for it.

TOSCA: Well I doubt if anyone picked it up, strides aren't always easy things to find, especially in front of gates!

Tosca saw no way to turn the conversation round to herself, but after a slight pause Prince Hal thought he'd better change the subject.

HAL: Have you had any good buttonholes lately?

TOSCA: I nabbed a super carnation the other day, but when it got half-way down, I discovered there was wire in the middle—that's why I've been off my feed lately.

HAL: Serve you right for being greedy. Talking about flowers, it makes my mouth water to jump at the White City.

TOSCA: Yes, it's lucky we're not like Ferdinand the Bull and just want to sit quietly and smell the flowers surrounding the jumps.

HAL: Do you remember at the White City last year when they had plastic ducks floating in the water trough that we jumped?

TOSCA: That's nothing, I was told there had been a rubber alligator in the water jump, only someone pinched it before the jumping began.

HAL: Extraordinary how foolish these course designers become. I suppose they keep the animals to float in the bath after the show is finished.

TOSCA: One thing amused me, were you at Rome when that foreign horse suddenly got nerves when he saw the water at the fence that the riders call the bidet?

HAL: Oh, I remember, his jockey took a header when the horse stopped, and after the mighty splash emerged draped with water lilies. I nearly bust my girth I laughed so much.

TOSCA: Actually I don't blame that rider for falling, because usually his horse is pretty stand-offish.

HAL: Yes, I've seen him stand off at least two strides from a fence and still get the spread—fantastic.

TOSCA: I'll say, he needs to be a bit of an athlete with the inaccurate way he's ridden. I just wouldn't go on trying at two fences out of three, if I was always asked the impossible or just left to make my own arrangements.

HAL: I know, I do like to be wild and free, but if I find that I'm left alone when I arrive at a large fence— d'you know—my heart just fails me. I wish my nerves could stand these speed events. All those common old horses can go in for the scurrys without a tremor, but if

[87]

I think time is going to count, my knees tremble and although with my thoroughbred blood I'm twice as fast as any of the other horses, I just seem to lose my head.

TOSCA: Can't hold your oats that's your trouble, old boy!

HAL: Speak for yourself, you were only given nuts last week, which can't say much for your great brain!

TOSCA: Brain? Why I even picked up my boots and gave them to Paul the other day. Admittedly she'd only just taken them off, but I thought I was jolly clever.

HAL: I bet you didn't think you were so clever that day when you were tied up in disgrace, after opening your own door and walking out all over the garden, and leaving your great hoofmarks on the newly-mown lawn. Mind you, I can untie myself. Talking of tricks, you should see that wretched little novice Oberon, getting all the attention. Anyone would think he was an Olympic Gold Medallist, just because he can bow when he wants a carrot. He ought to join a circus and not show off in front of us élite International jumpers.

Hal blows his nose in disgust, then yawns and turns his eyes inside out with a nonchalant shake of his head.

TOSCA: Well, when I tried to bend my knees like that everything cracked. I think it's a poor way of getting titbits. ⌣Anyway I don't need to look through my knees to see my beautiful tail.

HAL: I can't see your tail from here, but did you peroxide it this morning? I expect you won't have to bother soon if any more kids take a souvenir hair out, because you'll be bald. How did that pedicure go that the blacksmith gave you yesterday?

TOSCA: Better than the one you had in Nice.

HAL: Oh, *caramba*! (*showing off his Spanish after winning the Grand Prix in Madrid*). It hurts me to think of it. I don't see why this subject of sore toes should be brought up on Sunday afternoon—(*Slight pause*)—Do you know I love going round the country with you.

TOSCA: I think it's fun too, if you weren't so jealous.

HAL: Jealous! My off hind; I'm never jealous.

TOSCA: What did you say to Foxhunter when you accused him of nudging me in the parade at White City? I mean, one has to stand close to team members in these affairs.

HAL: I saw you fluttering your white eyelashes at him.

TOSCA: (*innocently*) Oh, no, I just got a little bit of mane in one of my eyes . . . and it wasn't Foxhunter that time, it was Ali Baba. You see one must show the *entente cordiale* to the visitors.

HAL: You fancy yourself with your French airs. (*He gives a forced yawn.*)

TOSCA: You lazy old thing. You can't even get up for breakfast, I like a man to get up for his work, and not go back to bed after breakfast. A fine time Paul has to get you up if we leave early for a show.

HAL: Oh, I don't mind that.

TOSCA: You do, you usually take a lump out of her.

HAL: Oh no, only if I get up the wrong side of my box, and then only very gently.

TOSCA: You vampire! I've seen you draw blood when you bite. *Paul appears and seeing them making faces at each other closes the box doors. Hal is heard to hum, 'The old grey mare ain't what she used to be'. However, the lady has the last word, as a stage whisper comes from Tosca's box. 'Vampire, Vampire, Va. . . .'*

[89]

CHAPTER 4

Olé! Olé!

WHEN I was young I did not think that I would ever go abroad, although I remember betting someone a thousand pounds, the largest imaginable sum of money, that one day I would go to the Argentine. I was riding Argentine polo ponies at the time and the heroes of my life were Mancha and Gato, Tschiffely's two Criollo ponies, that he brought from their native pampas in Patagonia, and then took them on his famous ride from Buenos Aires to Washington.

I was even writing a book, that never reached a publisher's critical eye, called *The Tale of a Polo Pony*. The names for my imaginary horses I found in a Spanish dictionary. This influence also came from the Spanish names of the polo ponies that arrived each year from Johnnie Traill's *estancia* in the Argentine. Incidentally, this book followed two previous ones, written in school exercise books, and possibly in school hours! The first was a great success, written when I was eight. It won a prize in the school inter-house handwork competition and was an illustrated edition of *How to train a Pony*. No doubt if this most clear and instructive work had been published, I would now be termed a professional rider! The second book was *The Story of Pixie*, my chestnut pony, who was four to my five years when we first met, and had been born and bred on Dartmoor. Without her help, I wrote of the happy days she had had as a youngster, and the freedom which she lost when a small girl started to inveigle her into jumping enormous obstacles. Neither this book nor the third was ever finished, as I decided that writing could be kept as a pastime for old age.

So not only did the ponies inspire me to some literary efforts, but without the horses I would never have had an opyortunity to travel, and to meet so many people. It is this mutual interest in horses that has given me the chance to make new friends abroad, rather than being suffered only as a tourist. Nationality makes very little difference between the members of the various teams, and I really enjoy trying to learn something about other countries and their languages. It is far more interesting staying with kind friends in a private house. Even when one has to stay at an hotel during the activities of a horse show one never gets the luxury of five minutes to oneself. Personally I find this a good thing, as perhaps I might lose any ability to make sociable conversation if I had time to brood on the problems of the forthcoming event.

Anyway, one rarely gets much intelligent conversation out of a rider before a big competition, especially if he is concentrating on some of the essentials—his horse, the fences, the turns in the course, the adjustment of his saddlery, his number and general turnout. Likewise, can one blame the rider for turning the other way when some stranger pushes a grubby scrap of paper at him for an autograph? For at that moment it is the rider's job to see that his or her horse is best prepared for the competition. It is part of his duty to the public to put up a good performance with his horse, not with his signature!

One of the disadvantages of going abroad is the accumulation of work at home. As the previous chapter has shown, I had quite a shock which quickly brought me back to earth when I returned from America. There were five large cardboard grocery boxes brimming over with unopened letters waiting in my room. These gave me the greatest pleasure to read, but meantime the horses were champing in the stables needing work. On top of this there were various social engagements which had to be fulfilled. The most impressive was the presentation of the Sportsman and Sportswoman of the Year Trophy at the 'Savoy'.

While I was away, I had not realized how well the Press had reported our successes during the autumn tour. From a complete lack of interest in our trials and errors of 1947 there had been very slight public attention in 1949, when the only headlines in the papers read, 'English Lady Goes Wrong Way in Paris!' This referred to someone taking the wrong course, merely because the horse chose his own route. There was no mention of one or two good British wins at that show.

Interest was definitely stimulated by the Olympic Games. First was the result before the closing ceremony at Wembley in 1948, when our team won the Bronze Medal in the Grand Prix des Nations. Then came that sensational moment in 1952 when we at home switched on our radio sets to hear the National Anthem being played on that final day at Helsinki. At once, we knew that the team had won the Gold Medal. This was in spite of the fact that the English had had their backs to the wall after the first disastrous round.

The wonderful effort of the people who sponsored our

American venture in the autumn of 1953 was luckily well repaid. The Press had given great credit to Prince Hal's success in America. From Hal and Tosca's consistently good results, I found, to my surprise and pleasure, that I had been elected the Sportswoman of the Year. People were becoming more interested in the sport of show jumping.

At home I soon had to start training the horses for the jumping events at Badminton in April 1954. The three-day event had already become very popular, with people coming to watch and bringing their cars and families from far counties. Combined training or *Concours Complet* as it is aptly called by the French, is the training necessary to produce the combination of the complete rider with the complete horse, able to cope with any situation or obstacle. The finished result takes much time and patience. Through the encouragement of Three-Day Events at Badminton, Harewood and the many one-day events throughout the country, Britain now has a team of really good horses and riders. They are trained for the combination of a dressage test, cross-country and steeplechase, with show jumping on the third day. This last test is really to show that the horses are still supple and obedient after the rigours of the middle day.

At Badminton, after the jumping test has been carried out and the winner has been found for the whole of the three-day event, other ordinary show jumping competitions are held in the main ring. The most important of these is called the Badminton Grand Stakes. Prince Hal and Tosca were due to jump, but I had some difficulty in getting them to the show. To my concern, I found that Tosca had slightly lost her nerve for travelling. If she felt that she had not enough foot room in the lorry, she would scuffle her feet until she nearly slipped down. After much patience, reloading with the horses in different partitions, and some extra smooth driving, Tosca settled down and we arrived safely.

Princess Margaret was watching the competition from a wagon in the centre of the ring. My first round was on Prince Hal, the hero of the American tour. He was jumping in great style when, true to the saying that even the mighty fall, he stumbled as he landed over a fence and deposited me at the foot of the wagon. Tosca made amends for this by going superbly, and winning on the timed jump-off. She received her rosette and was petted by the Princess. The following month Prince Hal more than redeemed his reputation abroad.

For the first time, a British team was being sent to Portugal before going to Madrid, where the Spanish were holding the World Championship. Along with Major Gibbon, Captain Dallas and Lady Mary Rose Williams, I had been invited with Prince Hal and Eforegiot. Eforegiot is a lovely bay, kindly lent to me for that tour by Miss Paget. At home there were hectic preparations for the long trip abroad. Not only was Tosca being left behind, but also some young ones, whose training programme would be interrupted until my return.

Before leaving England, Prince Hal won a test competition at Lambourn, home of many racehorses. Then the horses called in at the Royal Windsor Show for one competition *en route* for the ship. Actually it was Tosca who won this competition, although Prince Hal had

won it a year or so before. The international horses
acquitted themselves satisfactorily, and I picked up my
two from Windsor at crack of dawn the next morning.
Unfortunately, the silencer on the lorry had succumbed
to wear and tear, so I had to drive through the heart of
London to the docks well heralded by the deafening
reverberations of the engine. Even the horses objected
to this and were battering the boards just behind my head
with their hind hooves. I did not think that it was at all
funny until I saw the business men in the City holding on
to their bowlers and looking anxiously for the tank
battalion that was presumably invading their domain.
Once down at the docks, everyone was charming. We
were shown around the ship, introduced to the stewards,
and Prince Hal and Eforegiot were lucky enough to have
the same crates that had been used for two royal polo
ponies a week or so before.

Leaving them in the good care of Pauline, I went back
to Windsor, and then on to Trowbridge Show where
Tosca jumped in her best form, before being left in peace
at Miserden.

Practically before Tosca had cooled down from her
winning round in Wiltshire, I was driving to London
Airport to catch the Lisbon plane. It was exciting
enough to be flying to Portugal for the first time, but the
climax was to be in Spain, where the competitions for the
World Championship were being held.

After a great welcome at Lisbon Airport, we found our
horses well stabled in a private yard near the show
ground. Everyone was helpful and charming, and I was
in high spirits when we went that evening to the official
show reception. After meeting our hosts and all the

[95]

foreign teams, I found myself talking to a Spaniard. During the course of the conversation he casually remarked that of course I knew that ladies were not eligible for the World Championship competition. My heart dropped into my party shoes. This event at Madrid was to be the climax and aim of the tour, and as far as I knew my entries had been accepted. Further questioning, frantic telephoning, despair, and then a general despondency followed. There was nothing to be done about it, as apparently some international rule had been passed, and we had not been informed. There was the consolation that my horses could jump in all the other events.

It was impossible to ignore the blessings for long, and the next morning, after we had worked the horses, and the sun was beginning to compensate for its shyness at home, Senhor Graça, the owner of the house and stables, came out to talk to us. We were invited to sit in the pleasant shade of the trees, and to taste a variety of his delicious wines. At the same time we could watch our horses being groomed and cooled off. The grooms were playing a hose of cold water on the horses' legs to refresh and strengthen them before the week's jumping. We also had to decide on the entries for each horse, but before long we had drifted from the technicalities of show jumping to the intriguing hobby of our host.

He possessed some superb English greyhounds for coursing, and knew their pedigrees back to the original root of their family tree. I have a fellow-interest in greyhounds, as I had been given a young greyhound called Windy in 1950. Windy is a brindle bitch, with enough lurcher blood in her to become the most charm-

ing and attractive companion, an efficient and silent
poacher, and yet a sentimental friend and house-dog. So
our conversation warmed with the description of our
respective greyhounds, and after we had seen the kennels
we retired to the house to see photographs of the champion dogs.

My attention was caught by some of the tiled inside
walls, showing pictures of hunting scenes or designs.
Many of the better houses have outside tiling which,
like thatch, keeps the house cool in the summer and dry
in the winter. The houses are kept spotlessly clean with
this practical decoration. The tiles are called *azulejos*,
and besides being attractive they are tough, and last
for a long time. They do not need constant repair like
an English thatch. For a thatched roof is made from
material essential for birds' nests, and the birds will steal
the straw unless the thatch is securely netted.

Lisbon is a charming place, built on many hills, like
Rome. Looking out over the blue bay formed by the
mouth of the River Tagus, one could see all the little
sailing boats busy in the perpetual wind from the Atlantic.
The Gulf Stream does not flow along the coast of Portugal, so I was alternatively stimulated by bathing in the cold
sea and being baked by the hot sun. Then the controversy
arose as to whether swimming affects one's judgment.
If my eye was put out by springtime bathing under blue
skies, the horses were not so affected. They both jumped
brilliantly over the excellent international courses, and
they both won. I think that Hal's 'coup', the Six Bar
competition, was for me more exciting than any other
event so far.

It was held on a rather English evening, with grey

clouds and drizzle. Hal had never before attempted this rather specialist competition in which one faces a line of six straight fences with only two strides between each. To give him an idea of what to do, we rigged up a practice line outside the arena. The first time we tried, Hal jumped the first two fences with feet to spare, but as he landed over the second the third fence blew down in front of him. He stopped in a flash, and my impetus carried me straight over his head. At that moment my number was called from the main ring, and I had to remount Prince Hal without a moment in which I could brush off the tell-tale sand from my hat. We rode into the ring. I was worried and Hal was upset. Somehow we coped with that line of fences, only just managing to put in the two strides between each. For Prince Hal was fighting to gain speed, and I was trying to regain control.

Later by the time the fences had been raised for the third jump-off over three six-foot fences, he knew he was wonderful as he cleared the last with inches to spare, just before dusk fell on that rare damp day in Portugal.

One diversion during the show taught us the only sentence of Portuguese that we learnt during our stay. Little boys would bring choc-ices around the stands trying to sell their wares by shouting something that sounded like 'Askimovski'. When a rider wishes to make his horse take off for a jump, one uses the colloquialism 'to ask him off'. From the first day when we heard the youngsters selling their Eskimo ices, any rider who fell or hit a fence was severely told that he had forgotten to 'Askimovski'.

There was hardly a moment's peace for sightseeing in this charming and hospitable country, although one

day I was taken for the one-hundred mile drive to Fatima
to see the new cathedral. This has just been finished with
an impressive semi-circular façade of pillars, built on the
site of the miracle of thirty years ago. A vision of the
Virgin Mary appeared to some children who were
guarding their sheep and goats. Then a spring of water
on this site was found to have some power of healing, as
at Lourdes. I was impressed by the simplicity of the
tiny chapel where the services are now held for the pil-
grims, until the new cathedral is finished. In comparison,
this modern cathedral is not nearly so attractive as the
ornate stone work of the lovely old fourteenth-century
cathedral at Batalha. Portugal is rich in historical
palaces and interesting places, as well as the more modern
holiday resorts like Estoril with its flowered terraces,
villas and casino.

We were entertained at the casino one night after the
show, and I was shown the gambling-room with the
people at the roulette tables. The players were very tense
and I saw one large lady perched on a stool, raking in the
escudos with grim determination. I am sure that she
did not enjoy her win as much as I had enjoyed Prince
Hal's victory earlier that day!

I was also taken to a pinnacle of Lisbon, under the
Moorish castle, where one looks down on the old part of
the city, with its very narrow streets and unique style,
almost reminiscent of the Kasbah in Algiers. Then a
quick look at the famous collection of coaches, including
one that an English queen had travelled in to Spain.
This was not only superbly upholstered, with strong
and efficient suspension and springing, all camouflaged
with fabulously gilded figures, but it also had a modern

convenience fitted under the seat, which our guide took great pleasure in showing us! There were also some beautiful carriages built in London, superb examples of the craftsmanship of our coach builders in the reign of George IV.

Dazed by this galaxy of golden coaches, a reminder of the luxury of the Court in the past centuries, I wandered out into the sun. A friend and I walked over to the Jeronimos, the exotic and lovely Abbey of Belém. I had hardly recovered from the sight of so much glistening gold, when the blinding sun reflecting on the white limestone of the Jeronimos made me again shade my eyes as I looked up at the elaborately carved doorway. The fantastic and ornate double cloister left me in awe of the Manoelino style with the flavour of India, which may have come from the voyages of the Portugese navigators, Vasco da Gama started his sea voyage for India in 1497, from the nearby Tower of Belém built on the river Tagus with the waves breaking against its base.

As a wave receded we sprang on to the steps leading up to the tower, a landmark of Portugal. Before we reached the turreted top, we stood in opposite corners of a domed room in the tower and whispered to each other. The shape of the wall and ceiling carried the sound to the person standing in the other corner, without anyone else in the room hearing a sound. Portuguese architects must have specialized in this design, for the great Palace room in Queluz has a throne at either end, and yet the two Royal occupants of the thrones could whisper to each other, without their secrets being intercepted by the other courtiers in their presence. We left the orange trees and myrtle of the sunny gardens surrounding the lovely pale pink country palace of Queluz, and penetrated the mists enveloping the Moorish palace of Sintra. The two enormous conical chimneys towering above the Royal Palace, reminded me of giant Kentish oast houses. The tiling and the Moorish architecture brought back thoughts of the Alhambra at Granada in the South of Spain. Yet this Moorish influence has had quite different effects on the music of the two countries.

That night we were taken to a little restaurant in Lisbon to hear the typical songs of Portugal, the *fado*. While we sat drinking some local wine, *vinho verde*, and eating sunflower seeds, a girl stood up and started singing a melodious *fado*, to the accompaniment of a Portuguese guitar. She made up the lines as she sang, and another person got up from a table, to continue the *fado* in answer to her verses. This exchange of pleasantries in song was backed by the laughter and enjoyment of the people listening. The gentle music of the *fado* was very unlike the Spanish *flamenco* singing, with its wilder, blood stirring sounds. The guitars, being a different shape, also have quite a different sound from the Spanish guitar.

I was told that the *fado* sung in Lisbon was not the same as the type heard in Coimbra, the university town of Portugal. The love songs there are tuned to the romantic passions of the students, and the next day as we passed through Coimbra I was given a little china ornament of a boy with a guitar wooing his girl, both dressed in the colourful student costumes.

Carefully carrying my present, which survived the tour and is now here at home to remind me of Portugal and the *fado*, we joined the bustling crowds to see a little of Coimbra. After looking in the Sé Velha or old cathedral we eventually managed to find some dusty old carvings depicting the voyage of Vasco da Gama. These were in the organ loft of an old, old church, and were luckily one of the few relics that had not been renovated by eager restorers.

All these glimpses of the wealth in art and history were seen by us *toujours à la course*, freely translated as 'always at the double'. In fact, by eleven o'clock that same morning, we were already on the road for Madrid, chosen ground for the World Championship.

I was astounded at the speed and smoothness of the little '4 *chevaux*' in which we travelled. There were three riders and all their luggage piled into the tiny car, for a 450-mile drive over arid mountains and isolated country.

We passed through lonely villages, each with its church and large, untidy stork's nest on the tower. Perhaps this is the reason for all the small children we saw playing in the villages. I imagined I was back in medieval times when we came upon the walled town of Avila, looking strongly secure from any barbaric attack. The effect of the mottled bronze of the ironstone, and the beautiful proportions of the inside of this cathedral, gave me an impression of austere dignity. A feeling most fitting to the character of St. Teresa, who lived in Avila four hundred years ago. I had read and admired much about this Saint and her life became more real when I saw her home surroundings.

Then on through the Gates of the Lions of Castile and over the Guadarrama Mountains. Below us on the plains I could see the farms where the fighting bulls were bred, and I remembered three years before when I had held a cape myself.

The Madrid show ground had some new stables for the horses, and Prince Hal was in a comfortable box. He seemed to be pleased to be back in Spain, where he had performed in his first international show. He showed his pleasure by jumping with superb confidence, and ended by winning the Grand Prix.

I could hardly believe the result when it was announced that Hal was three seconds faster than any other clear round. I rode into the ring to collect his prize in a dream. The Union Jack was hoisted up the flagstaff, and the band played the National Anthem, unrehearsed, and in a minor key! I was presented with the lovely cup with the handles representing the Lions of Castile and supported by the bear—an emblem of Madrid.

On the national holiday of Corpus Christi, I was taken to Toledo to see the religious procession, and the fiesta bullfight. El Greco had lived in this capital of Old Spain, and painted some of his masterpieces in this ideal setting. Later that evening we were invited to an old monastery·on a hill outside the town.

There was little twilight in the evening and darkness fell very quickly. From the terrace we could see the outline of Toledo on its own hill, with the cathedral spire, the ruined fortress of the Alcazar, and the quaint old houses silhouetted in the moonlight.

At the foot of the hill glistened the silver ribbon of the river. As we sat on the terrace steps some Spaniards produced their guitars and played *flamenco* music. There was the scent of roses in the still air and before long, everyone was singing folk songs. The moon passed over the sky, and I was under a spell of enchantment.

The spell broke when Prince Hal lamed himself on

hitting just one fence at the show. I did not realize then that he would be out of action for the whole summer until October. Another slight setback for me at Madrid was a bug called the Madrid tummy. I had thought that I was far too fit to pick up this tourist affliction. I was told that my mistake had been made in drinking water from the tap when I was very thirsty one night. I had objected to paying more for a bottle of water than for a bottle of good local wine. The next morning I suffered the consequences and I staggered around feeling like death, only just managing to get to the show to watch the finals of the World Championship. This was bound to be a most interesting competition with four finalists who finished in this order: Herr Winkler from Germany, M. Jonquères d'Oriola from France, Captain Oppes from Italy and Commandante Gracia Cruz from Spain. There was an extra Spaniard in Señor Goyoaga who, a winner the year before, qualified to compete in the finals, and finished third between M. d'Oriola and Captain Oppes.

In the formula for the world championship the finalists ride each horse in turn round the course. They jump their first round on their own horse, and the next rounds on their opponents' horses. They are allowed about two minutes to get used to each new horse. During this time they may jump two small fences that are placed in the ring, prior to starting their round. After they have ridden each horse, their total faults are added up. However, they are doubly penalized if they make a fault on their own horse.

Some of the riders had obviously watched the horses that they were going to ride, and studied the style and method in which they had been jumped. Then during the two minutes when they first rode each horse, they had to adapt themselves to suit the horse and apply the few hints that they had picked up.

It is an interesting competition from the spectators' point of view, when they can study the application of technique. I doubt if it can be good for the horses, who are already stars in their own right and used to one method and one rider.

I did not concentrate much on the event as I was trying to stop myself fainting. I had not fainted since I was about seven years old, in church, and I staved it off until after the big event. Then I was supposed to receive from Generalissimo Franco himself the Grand Prix Cup that Hal had won the day before. Alas, I passed out just before the big moment, and before I was ushered through the cordon of his surrounding guards. As I was swept away I could hear the microphone in the distance persistently calling for me.

I had the whole of the next day in which to recuperate before the evening performance for the Nations Cup. Even then, after spending most of the day in bed, I was not at my fittest for this last competition in Madrid. I was feeling very sorry for myself when a friend rang to ask if I would like to see the famous Alba collection of paintings. It was a chance that I could not miss, so I dragged myself up. Looking at these masterpieces made me feel so much better than I managed to change into my riding clothes. The evening performance eventually began at 11 p.m., for time is unimportant in Spain. It was 3.30 a.m. when the final national anthem was played.

During the first round one of our team, Major Geoffrey Gibbon, broke a collar-bone in a fall, a disaster in a team event, and more than annoying for the sufferer.

By the time we were through with the transport and show arrangements it was time for me to have some breakfast coffee before visiting my kind friends at Monasterio. I had been there during the 1951 visit to Spain, and the Duke of Pinohermoso had allowed me then to play a young fighting bull with a cape. Again, this time, when we had driven across the plain that leads to the Guadarrama Mountains, we found the bulls and calves bred on the estate ready to test our bravery. The capes were produced, and after some of the polished performances given by the true matadors, we gave the toreros and the assembled company a little comic relief.

Yet more kindness was shown to me the following day, when a military car was provided to take two Spanish girl friends and myself to Segovia. I had planned an ambitious day which included seeing El Paular, the monastery hidden in the mountains, as well as seeing the great palace of San Ildefonso at La Granja before looking round Segovia. Our car must have divined my energetic programme—she started to boil anxiously while crossing the flat plain before the Guadarrama Mountains even came in sight. Places for water to quench her unassuageable thirst were few and far between. The driver was very philosophical about it, although he knew little of the workings of a car. Each time the car sang too loudly, we would stop and wait for the noise to subside. Then the radiator cap hardly needed a turn before a geyser of accumulated steam catapulted it across the road. There was no water on that mountain side, so when the cloud of steam had abated, the driver picked up the cap and screwed it on again. He shrugged his shoulders as he climbed into the driving seat and the car started. We found some water at a cottage farther up the mountain. I think that the car was past caring, but we must have saved her in time. While the radiator was being filled from a cup, which was the only available receptacle, a little donkey and her fluffy foal wandered up to see what we were trying to do.

With a great effort we managed to get over the Neva-cerrada Pass, stopping at the ski club on top to celebrate our successful climb and refill the car. Finding the remote way to El Paular was out of the question by then, but we had no intention of turning back. After another brief halt to remedy a puncture, the car regained her composure while we were coasting down the other side of the mountains, through peaceful and cool woods and glens. At last we arrived at La Granja. The palace looked immense and sleepy in the sun. We managed to wake up an old man to take us to see some of the lovely Goya and Flemish tapestries. Our guide loved his tapestries and proudly led us down hall after hall giving the history of each of the vast works draping the walls. He would barely let us go in time to have a look at the enormous but now silent La Fama fountain, standing in the great gardens of the palace. We had decided to lunch in Segovia, at Casa Candido under the great Roman aqueduct. This restaurant is famed for its roast sucking pig, a speciality of that province. There was no surprise when we arrived at four o'clock for lunch, and never have I had such delicious *cochonilla*. It fell apart as the knife looked at it, and then the meat of the sucking pig melted in the mouth, before being washed down by local Segovian wine.

After such a meal we were well prepared to appreciate the charm of the old-world town. We wandered through narrow streets, and saw the cathedral with its priceless Rubens tapestries, and the Alcazar, the fortress of Segovia, built like a great ship on a high table of rock. Below us was the old twelfth-century church of the Knights Templar, Vera Cruz, standing alone with its dignity and age and ignoring the height and impressiveness of the Alcazar. That evening we drove back a less exciting way, under the silhouette of a mountain that looked like a woman lying at rest. Back in Madrid we returned to a roof-garden, the guitars were produced and *flamenco* songs and music filled the still summer's night. I bought a guitar of my own the next day.

Before I left Madrid I had seen for the first time a *rejoneador*. This is the name for the man who rides his own superbly trained horses and fights the bulls from horseback as opposed to a matador who fights on his feet. I admired and was interested in the training of the fizzy little Andalusian horses for their dangerous work. A horse is naturally afraid of a bull, but these horses are trained to have such confidence in their rider that their obedience is complete, even when the bull is only a whisker away. They could perform difficult high school movements in front of the bull—then as the bull charged, it would find no horse in contact with its horns. The horse had responded to the balance and judgment of the rider. An expert, the *rejoneador* can keep the reins hooked on to his belt, and does not need them for guidance. If a complete trust and sureness had not existed between the horse and rider, the bull would easily find his target.

My introduction to this sport was through the *re-joneador* Angel Peralta. I had been taken one evening to the bull ring to see the museum with some of the gloriously embroidered capes of the famous matadors. While we were looking behind the scenes, seeing the chapel where the matadors pray before they fight, and the infirmary, white and sterilized to receive them if they are gored, someone came rushing up to us and said excitedly in Spanish, 'Angel Peralta has come.'

We went out to the yard to meet the famous *re-joneador*. His horses had already arrived from Andalusia, and were bedded down comfortably in boxes, resting from their long journey. The next day, riding these horses, his fight against a full-grown bull was to be the big attraction of the afternoon in the Madrid Plaza. The horses needed a little work to make them supple and obedient before their display in front of a critical audience and the dangerous bull carrying death on its horns.

Angel Peralta buckled on his leather trousers and rode each horse in turn, to get them used to the hard sand in the ring. I was surprised at the dexterity and suppleness of their paces, as they galloped and turned, twisting around the arena and gaily leaping in the air at some unseen movement of their rider. They obviously enjoyed their work as much as I enjoyed watching this display of horse-manship and the result of years of hard work.

The light had nearly gone by the time we left the arena and I was invited to join Angel Peralta with his manager, at a Bodega in the old part of Madrid. It was a meeting place of *toreros*, and they had to talk over the arrangements for the fight.

Later that evening we discussed the differences in the training of our horses, and came to the conclusion that in both cases all depended on the patience, knowledge and firm understanding of the trainer. He gave me a photograph of himself on a leaping grey horse, holding his hat above his head and no reins in his hands. A ferocious bull was nearby and there were tiers of spectators with anxious faces in the background. In return I was asked for a photo of Prince Hal jumping a large fence, but I pointed out that there was luckily no bull waiting for us when we landed!

We danced under the moon at the Villa Rosa. The first light of Midsummer's Day had appeared before we said, '*Hasta la vista*'.

I arrived at the Madrid Plaza in good time to see the parade of the *toreros* before the first bull entered the arena. The bull fight is the only thing that begins punctually in Spain. Angel Peralta was riding one of the greys that he had exercised the evening before. It was doing a graceful 'passage', the springy and suspended trot, that is one of the natural and beautiful paces of a horse at liberty when it is excited or showing off.

The first bull came into the arena like an express train, splintering the wooden barriers as it caught a glimpse of disappearing *peons*, the helpers of the matadors. Rafael Ortega was taking the bulls in an 'alternativa' with Peralta. The bulls were brave and Ortega fought well, but then the biggest and fiercest bull came into the ring for Peralta to fight.

He rode all three of his horses during different stages of

the fight, two greys and a chestnut. All were quite different and yet equally brave and fascinating to watch. My attention was riveted as he twisted and turned within a fraction of an inch of the bull's horns. Then he would deliberately gallop between the bull as it was charging and the barrier. As the horse evaded the horns, it would do a capriole, a leap and a kick in the air, as though it was telling the bull, 'You can't catch me.'

The bull stood for a moment, bewildered by the disappearance of the horse when its horns did not make contact at the end of the charge. At this moment Angel Peralta rode to the barrier just below where I was sitting and he reined his horse and took of his Cordoban hat. I suddenly realized that he was giving me the 'brindis' as he said in the traditional Spanish, 'I dedicate these bande-rillas to the beautiful and *sympatica* English rider.' With a 'brindis' can come the honour of a good fight, but if things go badly one also must share the blame. I was certain that nothing could go wrong that day and my hopes were confirmed as he galloped away and finished a perfect and brave fight.

The crowd cheered and shouted in their excitement and he was awarded the highest honour, the trophies of the ears and the tail of the bull. As he rode round the ring to receive the acclaim, applause, and a shower of coats and hats from the crowd, I threw him the carnation out of my hair.

I had to slip away before the last bull was fought by the other matador, as I had to catch the night train. I arrived at the station, depressed at having to leave Spain. Not only had I made good friends during the past week, but there was a festival of music in the open-air theatre at Granada, and I would far rather have travelled south to hear guitars in a romantic gipsy setting.

I was not allowed to brood over these last five minutes before the train left. Friends appeared on the platform from everywhere, including the young man from Panama, who had helped me to buy the guitar, with his music professor. He had always been able to play his songs from Mexico and Panama, but the professor had turned his interest to classical music as well. I was given one of the compositions that the professor had just written for the guitar. Then another friend from one of the embassies gave me an everlasting orchid, and someone else pressed a bottle of San Patricio sherry into my hands, some *turrones* were put through the window in case I got hungry and then—there was a scuffle of people at one end of the station as Angel Peralta came racing down the platform, closely followed by his manager. In his hands were the *banderillas* that he had dedicated to me and he had come to the station straight from the bullfight, so that I could have them as a souvenir of that Midsummer's Day.

Now, if my eyes happen to stray to the photograph that stands on my mantelpiece with the words written across it: '*Para la encantadora y simpatiquissima Pat con mi admiracion a su arte y escuela con la que ha entusiasmado a los espanoles, carinosamente,*' while I am dictating a letter or discussing the day's business, my secretary clears her throat and quickly reminds me that there is much work to be done.

I was not particularly looking forward to the third show of the tour, held in central France at Vichy. I was loth to leave Spain; Prince Hal was lame; and after an all-night journey it was cold and wet in Vichy. I was longing to get home to get on with a lot of work that had accumulated there. To cap everything, the Madrid bug returned for two days, and riding was painful with a damaged rib and shoulder from a fall. Through the show I only had the one horse to jump and although Eforegiot went extremely well, somehow luck was not with us, and he just failed to win until the last day. Then came the reward, when I was determined that Eforegiot should win the Vichy Championship. He was in great form and jumped two unbeatable rounds, thus finishing off our tour in a spectacular fashion.

CHAPTER 5

Grand Prix—Paris and Brussels

I WAS thrilled to get home, but found that Tosca was fat and unfit from her holiday. Then Prince Hal arrived back at Stroud station, and I went to meet him. I was certain that he would be better, but my heart sank as we led him out of the train box. He would hardly put his bad foot to the ground, and the usual stiffness from a long journey could not account for this. The White City, our most important international show, loomed ahead. I feared that Tosca would not be fit in time, and now Prince Hal looked a doubtful starter. The X-rays of Prince Hal's foot did not show much, but after a most serious consultation with Mr. J. R. Brain, our friend and vet for the horses during the past few years, we came to a drastic conclusion. Prince Hal had to have complete rest for at least three months. I had had great hopes of competing in Paris and Brussels during the autumn. Prince Hal was at the height of his career and in his element jumping indoors, but now it was doubtful if he would be right in time to get him fit for these exacting competitions.

Tosca came to the White City with me, although she had not had much work to prepare her. The first competition was the Selby Cup, which she had won twice before. Luckily she really enjoys the White City, and in spite of not being fit she tried her best and secured the lovely cup for the third time.

The honour of winning the Queen Elizabeth Cup has evaded me so far, and the next day we had this exciting contest. Tosca jumped faultlessly, and so did France's José Bonnaud on Charleston. In the jump-off on time Tosca nipped round the corners, and finished with a fast clear round. However, Charleston, last to go, galloped faster, and beat Tosca's time by a second. It was an exhilarating competition, and with the issue in the balance it must have been exciting to watch.

Our National Championships were held at Blackpool, and again Tosca seemed to be in terrific form. But again we went from success to despair, as she developed some gland trouble on the last day and nearly died of internal poisoning. She took a long time to recuperate, and was still uncertain of herself by the time Harringay came round.

Before Tosca completely recovered, I went to Jersey for a day, and watched a horse show there. I was thrilled to find an enthusiastic and flourishing pony club on the island, in spite of the children having far less opportunity with the limited amount of land, and the difficulty of finding new ponies.

A week before Harringay, Prince Hal was allowed to start work. I did not think that he would be able to jump so soon. Tosca, too, was a doubtful starter. She had not really recovered her confidence after her illness, and I was afraid she would remember her fall at her last indoor show in America.

Horses have long memories, but luckily Tosca has happy ones of Harringay. It was a risk to take the two horses to Harringay, but this time it came off. Tosca won the B.S.J.A. Spurs again, and Hal, after winning the

Diana Stakes, finished the show by winning the *Sunday Graphic* Cup, the Victor Ludorum Championship that Tosca had won the year before.

The rules of this championship ensure an exiting finish to the competition. The first round is jumped over a fairly big and long course. Then the jumps are altered to a test course with fewer and bigger fences. After the horses have jumped the second course, their faults for the two rounds are added together. This time there were five horses with no faults for jumping or time, so the fences were raised, and we jumped a third round. Our time counted on this final round if we were clear again. Dawn Palethorpe jumped a fast clear round on Earlsrath Rambler, who had been going consistently well throughout the show. Then came Wilf White on Nizefella, and in this round he wasted no time. He made the last turn as he landed over the triple bar, galloped to the last fence, taking off at an almost impossible distance from the wall. He was clear, and the crowd waited tensely for his time to be announced. It was half a second slower than Earlsrath Rambler's.

The crowd were still clapping the last horse as the bell rang for Prince Hal to start his round. I was over two fences before I heard people quieten and settle to watch the horse now in the ring. Although one notices the crowd's noise and reactions, I was concentrating on cutting every possible second off the time of our round. Hal was in great form, but he was nearly too excited to turn quickly after the triple bar. I thought that we had a second or two in hand from a quicker turn after the third fence— we galloped through the finish, I glanced up at the clock and saw that Prince Hal had won. What a compensation

After Switzerland, Prince Hal and Paul leave Miserden for Brussels

Prince Hal winning in Paris

My birthday in Geneva, with the cake of carnations presented in the ring

Leaning against Napoleon in Paris with Alan Oliver, Susan Whitehead and Pierre Jonquères d'Oriola

after months of doubt, and the fears that he would not be able to jump again.

Tosca and Prince Hal left for Paris with Pauline two days before I joined them there. During the weeks after Harringay they had had an easier time than I, but they were both fit, and in good form for the trip. Prince Hal especially had put on a lot of muscle with the three weeks of steady work. We were greeted in Paris with lovely weather. A further joy was to find the horses stabled in big comfortable boxes near to the Bois de Boulogne. Every other autumn we had competed at the indoor Paris show, the horses had not been stabled in luxury. Formerly, a storehouse had been converted into horse lines and the horses had to be tied up all the time. The horses usually developed coughs from the stuffy atmosphere, and they would not eat well. They could never rest peacefully with the noise of all the other horses, or lie down in comfort in their narrow stalls.

This had been the only place near the Vel d'Hiv, where the show was held, that could accommodate horses. With only a short time allotted in the morning for exercise in the small ring, it was difficult to give the horses enough work to prepare them for the evening performance. However, with the new arrangement and the comfortable boxes the horses were fit and happy. We could work them out of doors in the morning sun, and at night they were taken to the show. The articulated vans took six horses quite comfortably, although Tosca, being small, found the mangers a little high for her chin. The vans were built for racehorses like Prince Hal, so poor Tosca had to keep her head up while she was travelling.

I

Alan Oliver had also come with two horses, and on the second day of the show he flew back to Lancashire for his wedding to Miss Gene Whewell, before returning with his bride for a honeymoon in Paris and the rest of the competitions. The third British representative was Susan Whitehead riding the Hon. Miss Dorothy Paget's Scorchin'.

On the first day of the show, I worked hard with both the horses in the morning. I have always found that they need to be extra obedient for the first competition, because they are more easily distracted by the strangeness of the surroundings. As they settle into the routine of jumping every evening, often with tiring jump-offs, they need less work the following morning. Prince Hal is an exception to this, as he gets more and more energetic with more work. So a great deal of surplus spirits have to be worked off every morning.

The first evening's jumping gave a good preview of the general standard for the show. The fences were big and yet all the horses jumped them well. There was plenty of excitement for the 15,000 spectators packed into the Vel d'Hiv. The crowd is always sympathetic and alive, most of them going there regularly to see any sport that is on, whether it be bicycle races, wrestling, boxing or the horse show.

Tosca was over-anxious and too careful in her competition, and lacked the necessary zip for the speed that counted on the first round. Prince Hal's class was for the horses that would be competing for the Grand Prix later in the week. The course was made up of combinations of fences with one or two strides between each. There were four horses with clear rounds, and for the jump-off the fences were raised. The time counted on this round, and Prince Hal was first to go. He was clear again, but the other riders had seen the pace that he had set. They were also without a fault and only four-fifths of a second divided all our times. Prince Hal was fourth.

It is only a win that counts for international prestige although there was so little between these four horses. During the round the rider cannot afford to relax from complete concentration for a fraction of a second. One hesitation or slight mistake puts one out of the running, and even a perfect round cannot win a timed competition unless it is carried out with speed and accuracy. The rider has to be prepared to take risks, and it is an advantage to see the other horses jumping first, then one knows how many risks are necessary in order to beat their time.

The following evening, I nearly took one risk too many. It was at a time that mattered desperately as it was the first part of the Grand Prix. The twelve best horses qualified for the final of the Grand Prix, according to their results in three other competitions. The first part was a speed competition over quite big fences. I knew that the standard would be high, so if Prince Hal wanted a ribbon, we would have to do a fast clear round. Already some very good rounds had been jumped before my turn came. After jumping the first fence quite fast, I turned Hal quickly to save the distance before the next fence. It was not a difficult fence, but I had decided to jump it at an angle. Hal had sensed that this was a speed competition and was excited and unsettled. As we turned, he was fighting the bit, and did not see the fence until the last moment. His surprise made him stop, and

[119]

so a small risk that should have come off resulted in a refusal which lost the competition. We finished the round without touching a fence, but three faults for the refusal put us sixteenth in the final placing.

I was most depressed about this, as we would have to do extremely well in the other two competitions in order to get into the finals of the Grand Prix. In Paris, the only thing to do was to make the best of our unfortunate start. The next evening was free, so for the first time in my life I managed to get a seat for the Paris grand opera. The company were doing Weber's *Oberon*, with the ballet as well. The Opera House is an impressive sight, and every place was crammed before the curtain went up. With the opening scene, I found myself at the gates of fairyland. Two trees, standing like guardian dragons, showed the way to the gleaming white pinnacles of the fairy city. The ballet was like a dream and combined perfectly with the immense and beautifully dressed chorus. The splendours of the superb production reminded one of the extravagant days of Louis XV. After seeing the artistry of this performance and thinking of the work involved to produce such a fabulous combination of words, music and dancing, I went back to my job with renewed determination.

The next day Tosca was feeling herself on more familiar ground again. She was last to go in her speed class. The other competitors already knew their positions in the prize list, and Tosca had not shown enough form to worry them. However she did worry them when she scuttled round the fences, clear, and with the fastest time. The second part of the Grand Prix followed this and was again a timed event. I had one nasty moment when Hal thought he had to jump the left-hand of two fences placed side by side. We had taken off before I had persuaded him that our fence was on the right. He made an immense jump and cleared the right one. My heart was in my mouth, but we had achieved our clear round.

This pulled us up a bit in the general placing, but our final position depended on the Puissance competition. On that evening the show was being televised for the English transmission. The B.B.C., used to our big international shows of Harringay and the White City with the split-second timing of the schedule and efficient military organization, had not realized that time is immaterial at foreign shows. Instead of giving the English public the thrilling finish to this Puissance competition, the people at home saw fences being moved, raised, lowered and moved again. Eventually before our television closed down, a few clear rounds had been jumped and so qualified for the jump-off but the most exciting part was yet to come.

The competition ended with a final jump-off over three huge fences. The first was a high wall with a bar beyond it. Voulette, a charming grey mare, the French hope, ridden by M. Jonquères d'Oriola, who had won the gold medal at Helsinki, was first into the ring. She just hit the bar by not spreading enough for this high and wide fence. Then the large parallel bars needed accurate jumping without losing the necessary impetus for such a spread. The last fence was the test, a dead-straight wall standing well over 6 feet with no marked ground line to make the horse jump it well. There had been no clear rounds over this final course when Prince Hal's turn came. He jumped the first two fences easily, but he was fighting

with excitement when we turned for the wall. I
thought that we were a little close on the take-off, but
Prince Hal soared up and over to finish clear. Apart
from the lovely deep blue Sèvres vase for this victory,
he had ensured our place in the final twelve to jump for
the Grand Prix.

By this time I knew that Prince Hal was in such fantastic
form, that it would only be through a fault of mine if he
did not fulfil my ambition for the year by winning the
Paris Grand Prix. I felt my responsibility most terribly, and although one probably rides better when feeling calm and confident, I was tense and anxious. It is
only too easy to get worked up about these jumping
competitions. One is in the ring for about two minutes,
and yet I frequently think over that round for the rest
of the night. It is not only the winning round that is so
exciting. Sometimes a horse produces a complete
feeling of happy co-operation, and a joy of jumping.
Although through some small fault he may not have won,
the rider gets the utmost stimulation and excitement
from the round. At one show, I was thrilled with a
round that Tosca had jumped over a course that did not
suit her. We had not won, but she had done everything
I could wish for, and we had really enjoyed it. Somebody came up to me and said, 'What is the matter with
Tosca to-day?—not winning.' Luckily horses are not
machines.

On the night before the Grand Prix, the show did not
finish until the early hours. We had had no supper, but
I was ready for bed, to have as much sleep as possible
before the big event. *En route* for the hotel the others
decided that they were too hungry so we called in at a

bar in St. Germain des Prés. After having a sandwich, and joining in the dancing, I found there was little time left before I had to work the horses again. However, it was a lovely sunny morning for riding in the Bois, and I returned to the hotel at midday, where the draw for the order of jumping for the Grand Prix was to take place. The two prizes for the evening's competitions were being displayed at this official reception. I was afraid that something would go wrong with my round for the Grand Prix, so I barely glanced at the superb cigar box that would be given to the winner. The prize that really attracted my attention was a lovely clock, with figures of little jumping horses round the dial. This could be won in Tosca's competition, and our dining-room at home so desperately needed a clock!

In the evening we had two reception parties before arriving at the show. I think that I was concentrating more on the evening ahead than on the social conversation around me. When we arrived at the Palais des Sports I went to see the horses. Paul was getting Tosca out of the van, ready for me to ride her into the ring I was the first to go in the second section, so there was no hurry. After walking round the course, I was able to watch a few of the horses jumping in the first section. When I went to fetch Tosca we kept her as unexcited as possible. To warm her up, I trotted her down a side street, over the cobbles, away from the other horses. Then we were called into the ring. It was a touch-and-out competition with the horses jumping round the course until they made a fault. The winner had to jump the greatest number of fences in the time limit. Tosca was feeling in great form, and needed no winding up as she jumped fence after fence. Her time was nearly up; and she was very tired when I made a mistake and asked her to make too big an effort which finished our round. So far we were winning the competition, only there were still many more good horses to go. I could not wait to see the result of the other horses, as the Grand Prix followed immediately. Tosca was left in the collecting ring, and Paul took her saddle out for Prince Hal. I had to work him up and down a passage behind the Vel d'Hiv. He had been well drawn as eleventh to go out of the twelve horses. The only disadvantage was that he would be standing in the inside collecting ring, with no chance of moving until the other ten horses had jumped their rounds. Moreover the last of the twelve to go was the best of the French horses.

When Prince Hal had settled down outside, I rushed back to the arena, to see how Tosca's competition was faring. As I came through the door I heard a storm of clapping. This surely must be for a competitor that had beaten Tosca's time, I was certain that by then she was out of the running. I tried not to appear too anxious as I asked people who was winning the competition. Nobody seemed to know. The competition was over, and I still did not know the results. The soldiers were already changing the course for the Grand Prix, when over the microphone the prizewinners were told to come into the ring immediately. Tosca had won by jumping two fences more than the others. I rushed excitedly to get her, only to find that she had no saddle. She was too hot from her exertion and the stuffy atmosphere for me to ride her bareback, and after many gesticulations we managed to borrow a military saddle for her just in

time to collect our prize.   The dining-room at Miserden
was going to get its clock.

Prince Hal was waiting at the arena entrance as I rode
Tosca out.   I leapt straight on to him, and into the ring
for a quick canter before standing him in the inner collecting ring.   Then only a moment was left for me to
walk round the course, and size up the many problems
for this all-important competition.   Time seemed endless
while the ten horses before me jumped their rounds.
After seeing two or three times at least that Prince Hal's
tack was correctly fitted, it was time to get on him.   Once
in the ring he settled down quickly, and he was jumping
out of his skin over the fences.   There was never a doubt
about his clear round.   Several of the other horses were
also clear, and we all had to jump a second round.   Again
the wait, the agony of watching before going into the
ring again.   I had been misinformed that the result of the
Grand Prix was to be decided on the accumulation of
faults and time on the two rounds.   Prince Hal flashed
round with another clear.   His time was the fastest—
but no, he had not won, the microphone informed us that
two other horses that had also jumped two clear rounds
would again jump off with Prince Hal, with the time
counting only in this third round.   All the strain again—
the fences were raised, the air got hotter and dustier, the
horses were sweating, and I felt worn out.   It was getting
on for midnight.

The first horse in was the Swedish Lurifax.   Again he
went clear, and up went the Swedish flag, but I knew that
I could beat his time.   I took no risks, and Prince Hal was
clear again, almost wasting time in the air as he was
clearing his fences by so much.   He was several seconds

faster than the Swede, so down came the Swedish flag, and up went the Union Jack. The last horse to go was Vezelise. He had jumped brilliantly for Captain Guy Lefrant throughout the show, and was favourite for this prize. Vezelise jumped a fast round, but he was tired, and did not jump quite high enough. He finished with eight faults, and the Union Jack stayed in its place. Prince Hal came into the ring followed by Lurifax and Vezelise. The Anthem was played and I felt like following it up with, 'Why, oh, why do I love Paris!'

I very nearly missed the train to Brussels. The horses were safely *en route*, but I tried to fit in more than was possible before leaving Paris. The traffic did all it could to hold us up on the way to the station, but by the time the train puffed out, I was on it.

The Palais des Sports in Brussels has a larger ring than Paris, although in both places there is a cycling track around the outside. The conditions were the same for the horses, and we worked them each morning in the woods outside Brussels, where they were stabled. In the evening they were transported to the show by huge vans, and before they came into the inner collecting ring we could give them a canter in a small passage way.

Prince Hal was obviously in great form, and settled down to his jumping with sureness and enjoyment, but Tosca was not so happy in the soft sand of the arena. Her feet sank into the sand, making it more difficult to jump, and she was ready for her winter's rest. Of all the competitions, Prince Hal has never given me such a feeling of confidence as at this show. I had jumped at the show two years before, when Prince Hal and Tosca had won between them the Grand Prix de la Ville de Bruxelles.

This had been a competition with the rider jumping the course with each of his two horses in turn, the winner having the least faults in the shortest time. Tosca and Hal rather specialize in this partnership type of competition, having won the President of Mexico Trophy in New York, run on similar lines. So the horses had many friends in Brussels and people remembered them. One finds that any horse with a lot of character can make its personality felt with a crowd, sometimes even to the extent of getting fan mail and parcels of sugar!

It is always encouraging to a horse and the rider to have the crowd's enthusiasm. People are usually very fair, giving the greatest credit to the best performance, even if a foreign horse has beaten one of their own team. There are exceptions of course, just as the public at a bull-fight can turn against a matador. Then they force him into attempting the impossible, turning bravery into certain death. Too late, the people mourn the hero they have killed.

There was no hint of favouritism from the crowd when Prince Hal had his duel with Hicamboy, a Belgian horse. This was in the Puissance competition, when a reduced number of fences are greatly increased in size for each jump-off, until the winner is found. After the second jump-off, these were the only two horses clear. both good-looking chestnut geldings determined not to touch a fence. Hicamboy is a bigger horse than Prince Hal, but that was not to affect the issue. For the fourth round there were only two fences; first a straight red wall on the left-hand side of the arena, and then down the centre to an enormous spread fence, made of white bars on either side of an imitation bank.

The Belgian horse ridden by M. Poffé went first. To

the joy of the crowd he cleared both fences. Prince Hal came in. There was a hush from the crowd. He was pulling and fighting a little, as he still was not sure whether this round might be on speed—the possibility of a timed jump-off excited him terribly. I soon dispelled these thoughts of his by firmly keeping him in control at a slow canter before jumping the wall. In fact I had him almost too slow on the take-off, but in the last stride he crouched like a dog about to jump on to a high chair, and sprang over the wall with inches to spare. Turning for the spread fence, this control I had gained was more than necessary. There was the distraction of the 'way out' after the big jump; the gates into the collecting ring opened in a direct line after the fence. All horses are keener on the homeward journey, and these gates were an enticement. However, we were under control as we cantered down and jumped the fence to qualify for the next jump-off. Up went the two fences, the spread was widened, and the men were running about getting new layers to put on the wall. Into the ring went Hicamboy. He scraped over the wall, but it did not fall, and when he cleared the spread, in grand style, the crowd went mad. Prince Hal stumbled in the soft sand churned up at the corner of the ring, as I turned him for the wall, but as we approached it he settled, and was well balanced. After jumping it I turned for the last fence, and had the luck to sense the correct stride for the take-off as we turned. It could not have been easier. For the sixth round it did not look so easy. The wall was up to 6 feet, 6 inches and so was the last fence, which also added the problem of a 6 feet 6 inch spread. The jumps were high, the hour was late, and the horses were hot.

The battle was on, and Hicamboy faced the wall yet again. He cleared it and there was a 'shush' from some people to stop the crowd clapping in jubilation before he jumped the last fence. Alas, he could not manage the huge spread and he hit it badly. Hal was keen to get going, and there was a murmur from the crowd as if they were speculating on his chances. He jumped the wall, and turned nearly too quickly. For a moment he seemed too excited to be obedient, and it would be a very nasty moment for the rider if he arrived inaccurately at a fence of this size. Hal's courage was superb, and he used all his ability to gather himself, and easily cleared the spread. I felt as though we were diving down from the stars as we landed on the sand as winners of the Puissance.

The final competition was a high jump in place of the usual Grand Prix. Prince Hal was entered for this although he had never before competed in a competition of this type. Each horse is allowed three tries to clear the high jump before qualifying for the next height. The first time, with the fence at about 5 feet 6 inches, Hal was surprised to find that he only had one obstacle to tackle. He soon got the idea, and each time the fence went up he jumped it on his first try. By the time we reached 6 feet 6 inches we were getting a little anxious as to whether the poles would last out for a further height. The poles are specially made of padded bamboo, so that the horses will not damage themselves. So many poles had been broken by horses that could not quite make the height, that the carpenters had to start a running repair service.

There were only three horses left to face 2 metres 10 centimetres (6 feet $10\frac{7}{8}$ inches) and when Prince Hal

jumped it I was thrilled. Col. Llewellyn's great horse
Kilgeddin had cleared that height to win with me in
Paris. It was the first time since that night in 1950 that
I had competed in another high jump.

At 2 metres 20 centimetres (7 feet 3 inches) Prince Hal
again jumped it easily on his first attempt. He had won
the competition, so there was no need to ask more of
him. He also now held the official Ladies' European
High Jump Record. He was the leading horse of the
show, and with the points also gained by Tosca, he made
me the leading rider of the show. Prince Hal deserved
a crown. The greatest credit was also due to Pauline for
keeping the horses so well through the strenuous shows,
long journeys and hours of waiting in winter weather.

When the horses arrived back at Miserden they found
the flags out and 'Welcome' over their stable door.
The rain was dripping off the Union Jack outside, but
there was a good feed in the manger inside the stable.
They were worn out after their journey home, and retired
to bed soon after they had eaten their supper. The
next morning Prince Hal refused to get up, but condes-
cended to eat his feed off the floor while he was lying
down. He demanded the least privilege of a hero—
breakfast in bed.

During the winter the horses are rested. On fine days
they are allowed out in the paddock, where they give a
rodeo display of bucking, to show the joy of living.
They look so bonny and feel so naughty that I always fear
that their sense of humour will be worked off on me when
we start work again.

After the highlights of the shows, the star performers
become bored with their temporary retirement; but this

is the time when their legs can be rested, and they can forget the strain of the big competitions. They then come back to their work with renewed zest at the beginning of the next season.

The rider has no such rest. I can use this time to concentrate on finding and training young horses ready to start in novice jumping events in the spring. One cannot produce a top-class horse in a moment, and it is the hours of background work put in at home that count in the long run. Years later, one hopes to get the thrill and satisfaction from having the horse that has been trained at home, winning and jumping consistently. On the other hand, after all this work, one may find that the horse lacks some quality to make him a top-class performer. Then with patience, one must start training another, with faith that the result will prove more satisfactory. Life is never dull, for the more horses I ride, the more I learn how little I know. Success in any walk of life is never easily won, but in show jumping the work behind the scenes is always interesting and worth while.

An example of the kindness of the people in the horse shows abroad was shown to me in Geneva in November 1955. This was the big official International show with riders from ten nations competing and I was the only British representative with Prince Hal and the Hon. Mrs. Edward Kidd's grey mare Finesta. There was a painful first day with four of the girls competing having nasty falls including myself when Finesta tried to jump an artificial bank in the same way she had leapt over the jump before the bank—a water jump.

The next day Prince Hal and Finesta won the two-horse

competition, the Prix de Jura, and although we had
beaten a Swiss pair in the jump-off, the crowd had given
my horses a terrific welcome as they came in to receive
their prize. Later in the week in a competition for teams
of three riders, I joined two Swiss riders in forming an
Anglo-Swiss team. We were placed in the results and
after the prizes had been given I was astonished to see an
enormous 'cake' of carnations, bristling with candles,
being carried into the ring by a boy scout. The committee had somehow discovered that it was my birthday,
and before the horses were allowed to do their tour of
honour, Finesta and I had to blow out all the candles
assisted by cheers from the crowd!

After three months' rest, the same two horses came
with me to the Brussels Show held at the beginning of
March 1956. England was in the grip of the freeze-up
and it had been impossible to get the horses out to work
at home. In desperation I took them to friends living
near Windsor, for three days' work in an indoor school,
and Prince Hal had his first canter of the year only a
week before the first competition in Brussels.

In spite of the weather we arrived safely, with my two
horses far from fit. At a re-union luncheon, the riders
were welcomed to Brussels by the president of the show
and at the same time we were sealed into golden bracelets,
rather than have to argue with policemen at the door of
the show, as to whether one was actually competing or
not.

At the last moment it was announced that the doubles
and trebles competition with the jump-off against the
clock, to be held that night, would not count as the first
series for the Grand Prix as in the schedule. Instead the

Looking down at Les Baux

Angel Peralta

The cathedral at Bourges
at seven in the morning

One of the Gardian with
the Camargues ponies

Irène arriving at the chapel with her father

he Conte de Roux's Cabane in the Camargues

Flanagan's first outdoor international competition

At Algiers with Jonquères d'Oriola on Voulette, Paco Goyoaga on Fahnenkonig, and Hans Winkler. Behind stand a squadron of Spahis

Jumping M. Mathiot's horses at Lavarande

Ladies' competition and the Gentlemen's event, both over the same course on time, was to count towards the Grand Prix. This meant that the men had the advantage of knowing the time the ladies had taken in their event, if they wanted higher points towards the Grand Prix placing. Also, two out of the three events for the Grand Prix would be against the clock on the first round.

The first event for the second horses counted towards the Ladies' Grand Prix. In this the horses found the sand very heavy going. Only two horses did not touch fences, and Virtuosa, the winner ridden by George Calmon, had one refusal. The other horse Grispo Tusco was ridden by twelve-year-old Tedaldo Marzichi-Lenzi, who had special permission to ride in the Italian team. His classical style and excellent eye, with no hesitation when asking for a big take-off, earned him the crowd's admiration and applause not only because he was a little boy but also for his excellent round. This was only marred by two stops, one being caused by his brave and bold little horse stumbling in the deep sand and pulling off a shoe.

In the Doubles and Trebles there were three clear rounds, Prince Hal, Fahnenkönig with Paco Goyoaga, fresh and fit from his clean sweep of all the competitions in Berlin, and Tedaldo's father, the Duc Marzichi-Lenzi on Ventuno. In the jump-off against the clock, both the latter horses had the last fence down, but Prince Hal went clear again to win.

This first evening coincided with the *Horse and Hound* Ball in London, and I found Mr. Dorian Williams, my partner for the last three years at this Ball, commentating on the jumping at Brussels for the British television.

Later in the evening I was thrilled to receive a telegram from kind friends at the Ball, wishing me good luck. Their welcome message helped us throughout the show.

Although Prince Hal was clear in the first competition of the Grand Prix he was left standing fourth on time at the end of the first series.

The second round of the Grand Prix was over a bigger course on time for the first round. Prince Hal, second to go and clear, set a time of 51⅖ seconds, which was beaten only by Fahnenkönig, who in his hurry had a fence down. Apart from winning the event, Prince Hal then stood first on points in the Grand Prix placing.

On the night before the Puissance a gala ball was given at the Carlton with all the Horse Show people and competitors. The speaker, M. Jean de Faucon, produced a brilliant poem about the lovely ladies in the Quadrille display, which was the highlight to each evening's performance. During the night's entertainment Monsieur Smeets won the Coupe Perroquet for Belgium after a 'barrage' with Senor Goyoaga, for the quickest imbiber of a glass of champagne. Needless to say the British tradition was not upheld at this critical moment before the Puissance, when I merely raised my glass to the other concurrents, rather than drinking to their health to the detriment of my own!

The Puissance was the final event, the decider for the Grand Prix, and also the Grand Prix des Dames and Echarpe d'Or for the leading rider. Twelve horses qualified for the jump-off, after a first round over a stiff course. The course was then reduced to fewer and larger fences until by the fifth round, the French horse Camelia hit the red wall but cleared the spread jump, the only two fences left by then, leaving Fahnenkönig and Prince Hal without fault to fight it out. The wall at 6 feet 5 inches and the spread at 6 feet was then cleared by Fahnenkönig to the delight of the crowd. Prince Hal again was clear. The wall went up to 6 foot 9 inches and the last fence to 6 feet 6 inches with a 6 foot spread. Fahnenkönig could not quite make the height of the wall and took the top off, but then he cleared the last in great style. Prince Hal, still puffing from his previous exertions, came in to clear the wall well, and give the spread inches to spare, thus winning the Puissance. From this result, he also won the Grand Prix and the Grand Prix des Dames, although he had only competed in two of the four events that gave points towards this prize. This also kept the Echarpe d'Or for the leading rider in British hands and Prince Hal had completed his second Brussels show without touching a fence, last time having finished the high jump at 7 feet 3 inches.

The next day I flew back to Ascot, where Mr. Hanson's Flanagan was ready for me to begin the first day's training of the Olympic 'possibles' collected together at the lovely stables of the Windsor Forest Stud.

CHAPTER 6

Speaking of French, Three Falls and a Camel

APART from all the other well-known attractions of Paris, the horsy pursuits of racing and riding are within easy reach for the core of enthusiasts who live there. The Parisians are lucky to have the Bois de Boulogne for riding, with jumping paddocks at the various surrounding stables. Within ten minutes of the Arc de Triomphe, there are the racecourses of Longchamps and St. Cloud for flat racing, then steeplechasing at Auteuil, with the centre of the racehorse training establishments at Chantilly, less than forty-five minutes' drive away. In spite of this, most of the public who come to watch the yearly jumping at the Vel d'Hiv are regular customers. They go there in the evenings whether for wrestling, boxing, cycling or table tennis and with as much or more enthusiasm when the small arena is crowded with jumps, and the best horses of several nations are waiting their turn in the ring.

I have been jumping there since 1949, with various horses including Leona, Nobbler, Kilgeddin, Prince Hal, Tosca and Finesta, and now the crowd expects me to arrive at least with a grey mare, and most definitely with a white carnation in my buttonhole! Once the Paris crowd has accepted a rider, the performance in the ring, the trials and mishaps, the fortune and success are shared, felt and expressed by all.

After the atmosphere and 'ambiance' which I like so much at the Vel d'Hiv, I wondered how the Grand Palais would compare. This was the grander site for the official show in June 1955 and the first time since before the war that a horse show had been held there.

Prince Hal and Flanagan left for France while I was still at Richmond Show, jumping Tosca. On the first day Tosca won the Jubilee Cup and on the next day was one of the four clear rounds. I had to catch the plane for Paris that evening, but there was just time for the jump-off. This was on speed, and Tosca was going fast and clear, when in a difficult treble fence, where Red Star and Alan Oliver had just fallen, Tosca took one stride too few and fell badly at the triple bar. This was the middle fence, and I was not thrown clear, so as she bravely got up and jumped the last fence without me, she trod on my arm, a stud cutting into my wrist. I got on her again and jumped a fence so that her confidence would not be shaken, but I was not sure if my arm was broken.

After a quick check-up at the hospital, I caught the plane and arrived in Paris with a black arm swathed in bandages! The next day in the first competition Prince Hal realized that I was not at full strength; he was very difficult, but Flanagan was kinder. He enjoyed every minute of this larger arena and won three competitions during this, his first official International. Through the show as I got stronger, Prince Hal went better and finished with a brilliant win and a second in the Grand Prix being just beaten by France's Voulette.

In this Grand Prix there was a big double of wide

parallel bars. It was only possible to jump them fast with the horse full of impetus and made to take one long stride between them. Hal was clear in each of his three rounds, and as this was the final competition in Paris, the next time he jumped was in an English park.

On the way home we visited the Royal Counties show, and in the first competition there was again a double of parallel bars. He was jumping superbly and clear to this last fence, when suddenly he must have remembered the parallel bars in Paris, which he had jumped a few nights before. This time there were two strides between the two fences, whereas in Paris I had had to make him take one stride only. Now as we jumped into this double I was horrified when he took off again without the extra stride. He had nearly landed by the time we hit that last fence, and with the poles between his legs he had a really bad fall. It took weeks for the bruises to go. Both Tosca and Hal had fallen through making the same mistake and taking off too soon, although each time I had expected them to put in the extra stride. Also success in the Paris show had been sandwiched between two cracking falls for me, one in the last competition before leaving England and again one in the first competition on return!

In the spring of 1955, before the shows had started in England, I took the horses to the indoor show of Marseilles. Flanagan accompanied Prince Hal, so that he would get his first experience of international jumping without the strain of being in the team at an official show. I could thus put him in the competition that best suited him and ride with regard to his future, rather than having to win at that time.

The very first competition was for one rider with his two horses, riding the first one round the course and changing on to the second horse before jumping the course the other way round. Time and faults counted over a very twisty and difficult course, but both my horses went clear. Although their added times were slower than the winning pair of French horses, I could not have been more thrilled with their second place and excellent start to the season.

There was one 'diversion' between the competitions of the next day. Some of the competitors decided that they ought to get some dinner in the two hours' break between events. Nobody was quite sure at what time the evening performance would start, but one thing was certain, that by the time the show was over, it would be too late to get anything to eat.

The Vieux Port of Marseilles is surrounded with little restaurants where all the activities of this busy port can be watched as one sits at table.

It was decided that we should sample only the typical food of Marseilles, so the proprietors suggested *pizza* and *bouillabaisse* washed down by local *vin rosé*. The *pizza* is a very peppery hot and heavy flan, and the *bouillabaisse* consists of a soup with all kinds of sea food in it. We had oysters, mussels, pieces of big fish and little fish, together with rounds of bread to sop up the soup. All was well flavoured with garlic and by the time we had finished, I very much needed the coffee to take away the taste! Everyone could hardly move after this feast, but I was worried about the time that was passing, unnoticed by the others.

Eventually they realized the hour and we all bundled

into the car. Back at the stadium, there was a deathly hush as we came in. Apparently the crowd had been waiting half an hour for us. The committee could not start the show without the leading competitors, and more important than this, the competition was a 'knock-out' one. In this the riders competed against each other in pairs, with the respective winners qualifying for the next round, until the winners of the semi-finals met to decide the competition.

One of our party was in the first pair and his groom was holding his horse by the entrance of the ring. He had not seen the course, and as he wandered in to look at the jumps dragging his red coat in the dust, the crowd gave a few slow hand claps. Undeterred he mounted and proceeded to win the first round and continue unbeaten throughout the competition. It says much for the strengthening qualities of the *bouillabaisse*, that of our party of four we were placed first, second and equal third.

On Palm Sunday we were able to go to the Church of Sacré Cœur to hear the Mass of St. Hubert, the patron saint of hunting. The six huntsmen blowing the horns were expert and the whole service was dominated by the horns, which at one time resembled the ringing of the changes with church bells. The sermon was especially for those interested in hunting and horses, although all the vast congregation listened attentively.

Afterwards the scene changed as we were rushed to the Palace of Varieties to be interviewed in front of a crammed audience, with Tino Rossi following us on to the stage as the next attraction.

When the show had finished, there was time to spend

a pleasant day at Toulon, making my acquaintance with the British, French and American Navy, apart from having my first glimpse of the bathyscaphe used in deep-sea diving.

I then had to leave the hospitality of the people of Marseilles and join the other riders at the airport to catch the plane for Algiers. It was night when we arrived over the bay of Algiers with the lights twinkling along the coast.

The horses came by sea overnight and they had an eventful crossing, with some poor fellow trying to commit suicide by throwing himself off the boat. However, he was spotted and the big boat turned back. After he had been more than an hour in the water, he was rescued, more dead than alive.

Algiers Show was again held in the Hippodrome on the racecourse, with a selection of some of the best European riders. Amongst these were Señor Paco Goyoaga, World Champion in 1953 and the winner of the Gold Buttons and the Grand Prix d'Alger at the last show in 1953; Monsieur Jonquères d'Oriola winner of the Olympic Gold Medal at Helsinki and the World Championship in 1952, Herr Winkler, World Champion in 1954 and 1955 and Georges Calmon, Champion of France.

On the first evening before the show opened, there was a big reception in the huge tent that housed the horses. The Governor-General of Algeria and our Consul-General inspected the lines of smart horses, with the grooms standing beside their charges. Each horse had his name and his country's flag over his stall, and at the far end of the line of famous horses was a larger tent prepared for the reception. Here, amidst a galaxy of flowers and colour, the riders were introduced and welcomed to Algiers.

On the first day Flanagan was clear to the water jump. This was not big, but it was the first time he had seen one. As he was in mid-air, he glimpsed the water and dropped a front leg straight down into the depths. He rolled over and trod on my leg and foot, laming me considerably although luckily he was all right.

Poor Hal very nearly took a voluntary in the next competition when he tried to bank the thick green hedge which divides the arena and has to be jumped once or twice in each round. It is difficult for a horse, in the tension of a competition and ready for the possibilities of meeting strange fences on the first day of an international show, to differentiate between a solid-looking green fence and a green bank.

It is impossible to fly a bank without a disaster, in fact two bad falls that I have had at banks have been through the horse trying to clear the bank without putting its feet on top! It is equally impossible to try to change leg on the top of a green hedge. However, Hal did not fall although he bruised a leg on a pole.

The next day being Good Friday, we all had a rest and most of the riders were taken to the lovely country house and estate of Monsieur André Mathiot, the president of the show. The first part of the 100-mile drive took us by the coast. The other riders decided that I needed to stand in the sea, good treatment for my swollen foot that had been under Flanagan's great hoof the day before. As we always use this remedy of sea water for our horses whenever possible, I agreed to their suggestion.

We fought our way down through prickly cacti and wire grass to the shore, where I left my shoes. I cautiously stepped into the cold but calm sea, and picked my way from rock to rock, carefully avoiding the spiky sea urchins. A little way out I found a comfortable rock to sit on, just out of reach of the waves. I could see the others collecting sea urchins, considered a delicacy for our lunch; though later when I saw these *oursins* opened, the sight and taste did not whet my appetite. The rest of the party started going back to the cars, and by the time I had paddled to the shore, I had found on the way, when the seventh wave came, that I had not rolled up my trousers enough, and then that my shoes had disappeared from the beach. It was open to question whether the good done by the sea was worth the agony of the prickly track up to the road! My feet were not as tough as the little Arab boys', who could run barefooted on any surface. Once on the hard road surface I was able to deal out swift retribution to the thieves and retrieve my shoes, before we continued on our way to spend a pleasant day in the country.

The highlight of the show was on Easter Day when more than 10,000 spectators gathered to see the Grand Prix d'Alger, with the coveted set of gold buttons for the winner. Two rounds had to be jumped, with the second course as for a Puissance. In the case of equality of faults the times for the first two rounds were added together with the faster time winning.

Over the first course, Prince Hal came near the beginning and jumped a fairly fast clear. Whether the other riders tried to jump the course too fast, or else the difficult last fence of a big treble accounted for much of the trouble, there were no other clear rounds out of the twenty-four qualified horses.

Over the Puissance course Prince Hal was again clear ensuring his victory and the gold buttons! The final result was represented by four nations, with Monsieur Jonquères d'Oriola on Voulette second, Señor Goyoaga on Fahnenkönig third and Herr Winkler fourth and fifth. Two years before the same three riders with order reversed were placed in the Grand Prix, with Señor Goyoaga winning on Vergel, Monsieur d'Oriola second on Aiglonne and myself third on Monty, who had been kindly lent to me by Col. Llewellyn for the show.

Before the Grand Prix there had been a parade of the Nations and qualified competitors with the famous band of the Foreign Legion playing the national anthems. Although it was nearly dark at the end of the competition itself, the presentation of the Grand Prix was sensational. A squadron of spahis led the way into the ring, and then came Prince Hal, followed by another squadron of spahis mounted on their dashing grey Arab stallions. In front of the jury the other prize-winners were brought in, and the horses had a mouthful of oats as their reward, while the rosettes were being distributed.

The Grande Finale of the last evening was the Puissance, with four horses qualifying for the jump-off in the first round. Eventually in the dusk, Prince Hal beat Herr Winkler on Halla with Flanagan showing most promising form to be placed third. Thus the Algiers Show closed on the notes of our National Anthem and I returned home to start getting Tosca fit for the English shows.

II

Little did I think at that time when I tentatively accepted the invitation to join in a private jumping championship, that this would lead to spending two days of the New Year one-third of the way between Algiers and Timbuctoo.

The kind invitation of Monsieur André Mathiot, President of the Algiers Horse Show, was to the three world champions, Paco Goyoaga of Spain, Pierre Jonquères d'Oriola of France, Hans Winkler of Germany and myself, to come to his home of Lavarande. There we would hold a show on four of his horses and afterwards fly down to the Sahara for a change of mounts—camels. I duly arrived on the prearranged date, after a pressure of cables from Algiers and letters from the other riders, only to find that they had cancelled their air tickets the night before, partly due to the scare of rebels.

However, I was given a great welcome and after a day in Algiers I was taken off to Lavarande, driving over the lovely mountains, and keeping open a wary eye for bandits. I imagined I was back in the days of Monsieur Mathiot's great grandfather who always kept his pistol by his side and lived the same life as the Texans of the time of Davy Crockett. In fact the settlers of both countries were having roughly the same troubles in the eighteen-thirties.

The horses were brought out next morning—they were a grand type of big Anglo-Arab, with plenty of substance.

[145]

My fitness was tested as I rode and schooled them one after the other. Heavy rainfall the previous week had turned the jumping ground into a waterlogged and muddy bog. As riding on this 'terrain' was out of the question, I worked the horses on the small circular and sandy drive in front of the house. This proved to be good though firm ground, with the added excitement for the rider of ducking under a weeping willow, and then trying not to knock the oranges off an orange tree with a toe while avoiding a cactus and a palm tree on the other side.

A jump was erected a few feet from the willow tree and after preliminary work at a trot over a low bar and then two bars about a yard apart forming an oxer, we really got warmed up. Great was the excitement of the Arab groom, Abadah, when each horse jumped between 5 feet 6 inches and 6 feet without a mistake in two day's work. I am not sure who was the most surprised, myself, the owner or the horses. One young horse was initiated into the joys of jumping and took to it like a bird to the air. So powerful was his leap in fact that I was nearly catapulted off when he jumped 5 feet high over a two-foot fence out of a trot. In fact each morning's work was a tremendous success and I enjoyed every moment of it, for here were horses that with a little schooling could go into top international jumping.

Just as I had finished working the horses, the quiet air was disturbed by a vibrating noise, like the magnified sound of a diesel lorry. The coloured birds, that had been singing an accompaniment to the clip-clop of my horse's hooves, flew away in fright. A helicopter appeared over the orange grove and came and hovered above the house. Monsieur Mathiot did not know much about this apparition, but it went and settled in a field by the drive.

The French pilot came across the garden, and introduced himself as the liaison between the troops fighting the bandits in the hills. He had seen this house from the air and thought he would come in for lunch. We all walked into the house, and another place was laid for our new friend. He obviously had a fairly free life, with the independence of his helicopter, and any estate within a hundred or two kilometres was an easy distance for a neighbourly visit and a meal.

We had a very good lunch with local white and red wines grown on the estate, and we finished with *turrones*, the delicious compressed nut slabs especially eaten in Spain at the time of the New Year Celebrations. I had been given these in Madrid, where I had changed planes and lunched with some friends, on the way to Algiers.

With the coffee and *marrons glacés*, there was also cognac. Our flying friend said that he would not have too much of the latter as he held out his balloon glass for the second refill. He told me that he never drank much when he had to fly, and asked me if I would like to come for a little trip with him after lunch. I was obviously expected to go, so out we went to the helicopter. It was drizzling by then, and the tracks to the field were very muddy.

I climbed up and strapped myself into the bucket seat. I felt like a goldfish in a glass bowl, but I was surprised and relieved at the apparent simplicity of the controls. The right buttons were pressed and we started vibrating noisily with gyrators whirling round and creating enough wind to blow poor André back into the house. With great co-ordination we left the ground and the pilot insisted on demonstrating his steed's manoeuvrability only a few feet above the muddy ground.

Suddenly we shot up two hundred feet into the air, and although the glass cabin was spotted with rain drops, I took a few photos of André's establishment below us. The pilot then told me above the roar of the engine that he was leading an exciting and dangerous life, but he was lonely and looking for a *sympathique* wife. The life was good and there was always the freedom of the helicopter. Perhaps it is just as well at this height that I did not say *oui* to the sixty-four thousand dollar question.

After my tour, our friend flew off into the blue with his helicopter, wishing us a farewell until the following week-end, but we did not see him again.

True to the original promise, we then flew into the heart of the Sahara. After getting up at 4 a.m. we found a crowd at the airport all waiting to catch the desert 'milk-plane'. With a load of freight and sixty-eight passengers, the plane took off slowly and spiralled up through the rain over Algiers, until we saw the red dawn over the Atlas Mountains. Once we were through the cloud and our course was set south, we saw nothing except for white puffy clouds below, and thin grey cloud far above. Once, the long bare back of a desert mountain appeared beside us, alone in the sea of clouds.

Nearer our destination of El Goléa, a remote oasis one-third of the way between Algiers and Timbuctoo, the low cloud disappeared and gave way to vast stretches of sandy ridges and black-topped desert cones. There was not a sign of life anywhere and the first mark of civilization

El Golea—
Piccadilly Circus

By camel

Jumping Oberon

Jack Talbot-Ponsonby talking with Harry Llewellyn

Prince Hal winning the Grand Prix
of Madrid, 1954

Who's stolen my shoes?
Algiers, 1955, with Bertrand
du Breuil

Tosca at the White City

Talking to Crown Princess Beatrix and Princess Irene of the Netherlands at the White City

First past the post—on a donkey

from my side of the plane was the sudden appearance of the runway as the wheels touched down.

We were greeted by the cold dryness of the desert wind and I realized why the tough-looking men in the plane were all wearing Canadian wind jackets with furry collars, and why the Arabs shielded their faces with the end of their turban. After a few moments I looked around and all the gold-diggers—or petrol-seekers in more modern terms—had vanished into the desert. I just caught sight of four burly fellows climbing into the back of an old army lorry, although not nearly so nimbly as an Arab in his baggy trousers who found a sheltered place behind the cab. As the lorry jolted off towards the high plateau beyond the village the four from the plane were still groping for their suitcases to sit on. This was the last I saw of any of our fellow passengers.

An airport van took us the short way to the centre of the village, a huge and empty square of sand. I wondered where the village began, when it dawned on me that the sand walls, which I had thought were ruins, were actually Arab houses. The Arabs themselves were much darker than those of the north, with half the population of a different origin and completely black.

There were one or two blanketed Arabs asleep in the shelter of the walls and we passed one elderly man wobbling down the road on a bicycle with his trousers, blanket cloak and girdle billowing in the wind, dangerously near the spokes of the wheels. The van drove through some narrow gates just by the market square and we pulled up between an old pump and a circle of Arabs sitting in the sun.

We wandered doubtfully across the deserted yard to

the only hotel wondering if we would find anyone at home.   Our doubts were dispelled as we came through the rounded archway into a wide passage, with the grey walls draped with blankets and coarse carpets, worked in the cheerful Arab colours and patterns.   There was a roaring fire in the grate at the far end of the passage, and when mine host came forward, he greeted us with pleasure and astonishment.   Then he said that he had seen me winning the Championship at the Vichy Horse Show in 1954.   The desert is but a small place.

El Goléa has only recently been linked with Algiers by a regular air service, through the interest of oil companies in the possibilities of the desert.   But because of its complete absence of tourist attractions, it is the most typical and unspoilt oasis within easy reach.

Our host promised to give us anything but a desert lunch, thanks to provisions brought in by air and a good French cook in the hotel.   Before this was put to the test we had plenty of time to explore the village.

As soon as we set foot outside the hotel two young Arab boys attached themselves to us, and before we had reached the far side of the market place we had collected a small following.   A boy of thirteen, who spoke excellent French, elected to be our guide.   He and his friend, much darker than himself, worked hard to disperse the rest of the boys, and in no uncertain terms the hangers on were sent packing.   Most of the children talked some French and all the Arabs we met had charming manners.   We were greeted as they passed by, with a friendly 'Bonjour' or 'Salem Alikoum' and 'La bess'. The whole feeling was as different between the north and the traditional politeness of the southern Arabs, as one

finds in America with the friendly coloured people of
the southern states of the U.S. compared to the more
reserved approach in the north.

I wondered where our young guide had picked up his
Parisian French, and he told us that most of the children
were taught by a '*père blanc*' who ran the school there.
This bearded monk had proved his brilliance as a teacher
with all the children speaking such fluent French, although they had little chance to contact other Frenchmen.

We strolled between the high sand-brick walls built
round the Arab properties. Each family enjoys its
entire privacy and the walls are built high enough to hide
their patches of corn and their shelters from the eyes of
outsiders; although some of the walls had crumbled
when a rare shower of rain had fallen the week before.
Around the puddles still lying on the hard paths the
slippery sand was dented with the hoof-marks of camels
and donkeys.

We walked through a gap to talk to a friendly donkey
tethered to a bush, who proved himself most photogenic
when posing with the boys. Brown birds with white
tails, called *tourterelles*, skimmed among the palm trees
out of range of the stones thrown with great accuracy by
a small black boy.

We picked our way round an irrigated patch, and were
tactfully told that we had better retrace our steps as we
were on private property. As a compensation we were
proudly shown 'The Fountain', which consisted of crystal
clear water flowing out of a concrete wall along a small
concrete trough. Lower down the trough the water
cascaded into an attractive stone fountain where young
children were washing clothes.

Above the village, lying under a high mound topped with two great rocks, we found the cemetery of the French soldiers who had died in the battles fought at the turn of the century. From this silent and stony hillside we had a wonderful view across the village, to the great ruins of the Vieux Ksar, a fortress built on the opposite hill. Beyond this was the long cliff leading up to the plateau. The lovely shades of the green trees and the corn, and the rose, mauve and grey green of the sand, were soft colours one could see only on a grey day such as this. A true painting of the scene could be believed only by people who knew the desert in this mood.

I stood enthralled listening to the silence and absorbing the beauty of the colours. The stillness was only disturbed when the boys brought me shells and fossils from bygone ages, formed when the Sahara was a vast sea. Our guide said that if I could wait a moment he would fetch me two spiral shells from his nearby home. He then removed his old and laceless gymshoes and ran barefooted across the sharp rocks and stones, waving a shoe in each hand as he disappeared behind the hill. A few minutes later he returned and breathlessly asked us if we would like to have tea with his family. We did not have time to take advantage of this charming invitation, so he came back with us to the market place.

On the way we gave some coppers to an old blind man stepping high and led by a small black girl. As we walked on we heard a terrific 'discussion' in Arabic and our interpreter told us politely but with a broad grin that the old man was saying the equivalent of *comme vous êtes gentils*. It did not need much imagination to understand the pathetic snatch and grab and accusing shouts going on between the old man and the young child. However, all the other Arabs we had seen looked cheerful and content, although there seemed to be no work to do. We asked our guide what he did all day now that he had left school. He thought for a time, then shrugged his shoulders and smiling said, '*Rien*'. Then he added as an afterthought, 'One can garden'!

He showed us some of the orange groves, and the plantations for dates. All the palms had a few dates on them, although the harvest had been collected some time before. This ensured that the gardeners always had something to eat and could shin up a tree to collect a handful of dates for lunch.

Unlike the more prosperous oasis of Tourggourt, famous for its export of dates, El Goléa used most of its produce for its own people. The Arabs live on oranges, dates and *couscous* made from ground date-stones. They supplement this with any vegetables they can grow and occasionally meat from gazelles, sheep or camels, though the last is fairly expensive. The Moslem religion forbids them to eat pork or to drink any alcohol, an understandable law when the large families live in very close quarters. The other practical rule of life is that they must wash and be clean before they pray at the five ordained times a day.

In one enclosure there were a few chickens and a shelter with a wire-netting run. Behind the netting was a tiny gazelle that looked at me with big weepy eyes, and had as a companion a hairy little goat with shaggy trousers. The market place was empty except for one camel and one donkey, both asleep in the sun. Beside a wall there were a few Arabs crouching on their heels or sitting crosslegged around something cooking on a fire. We took the hint and returned to the hotel for lunch. There, we bade our guides adieu, rewarding them for their kind attention.

Although I was hungry, the meal exceeded all expectations. There was dried ham to start with, followed by a delicious mixture of vegetables and pimentoes which I thought must be the main course, until a further steaming dish arrived. This proved to be a hotpot of gazelle, with more flavour than venison or jugged hare. As I ate it there was a crunch of sand in each mouthful. This was not unpleasant and no doubt very good for the teeth and digestion. I imagined that after spending a few weeks in the desert the habit would grow and one would ask the waiter, 'Garçon, a little more sand please.' We rounded off this wonderful meal with a cheese soufflé and then delicious fresh oranges were placed on the table. They were pipless, small and with an excellent flavour, probably due to the lack of moisture in this region. The final 'pièce de résistance' was the best coffee possible.

We reclined on couches covered with Arab rugs, with the coffee within easy reach on camel-hide poufs. While we were waiting there, a friend of our host arrived with a Land Rover. He kindly took us to see the cathedral which was a little way out of the village and used only on very special occasions. From there, we drove up on to the plateau, skidding up the slippery cutting. I took my hat off to this vehicle, as it had to navigate the impossible desert tracks at speed, so as to jump the worst of the hard ridges.

After looking down on the tiny oasis surrounded by

the vast and desolate Sahara, I gladly got back into the Land Rover and out of the cold and penetrating wind. The Land Rover left us at the bottom of the Vieux Ksar and with darkness falling quickly I did not climb up to explore the old ruins. So we walked back through the Arab cemetery, among the children playing there.

A caravan of camels was arriving at the market place in the dusk. Arabs appeared from nowhere to join in this one excitement of the day. The 'Centre de la Ville', which had been nearly empty all day, with the bright and gay garments worn by the Arab girls, suddenly became a scene of action and colour.

That night we had far better entertainment than any television programme or revue could have given us. Our host was the best 'conteur' of stories that I have ever heard. He had been a director of the Opera in Algiers at one time, and now he produced flawlessly any dialect or accent for his stories, of which he had a list of six hundred and ninety-eight. Instead of an early night we listened absorbed until the diesel engine stopped generating electricity after midnight and we had to grope for candles and matches in order to find our rooms.

The next morning, as soon as I had donned some black baggy trousers, with white embroidery down each side, my camel arrived at the door. This was no ordinary camel but a pure white Mehara, from the troop of mounts of the Meharistes or desert patrol. I removed my shoes before mounting his berugged hump surmounted by a *rehalla*, reminiscent of a saddle. Instead of using improvised rope stirrups on either side, as with ordinary camels, I was told to cross my bare feet in front of his hump and I rode as a Mehariste.

As soon as I was aboard, the Arab made a hissing noise and my camel heaved to his feet like a ship in a rough sea. I knew that this camel was no ordinary one, and I soon found that not only was I aloft on his hump and aloof from all contact, except where my feet rested, but he was obviously sensitive and highly strung.

The first crisis was caused by an army lorry, rudely vibrating across the desert square, shaking the sandy walls and confirming that my camel was not traffic proof. By the time we were walking with a thoroughbred and long springy stride along the narrow track leading to the airport and the Sahara, a jeep and an ambulance van chose to dash by. My camel shrunk his hump so that the *rehalla* slipped slightly to one side and he tried to camouflage himself in the palms and sand dunes which he saw in the distant security of the desert. Meantime I saw drops of black sweat forming behind his ears, although this was nothing to the dampness, fanned by the cold wind, that I felt down the back of my own neck.

I am sure that anyone who is used to riding and being perched up on a high horse, would take quite kindly to camels. The greatest difference I found was the lack of direct contact. A rider has a horse between his knees and a change of balance or direction can be immediately indicated. In a moment of insecurity the rider can even hold on to his horse's mane, but a camel's neck is well out of reach. Sitting aloft on the pyramid of a hump, with only one rope to guide him by, I felt I would be more fully equipped if I knew some Arabic camel commands.

While we were loping along, I found myself humming, 'The camel he said sit down, sit down you're rocking the boat,' But in most of the pictures of people galloping on camels, the riders never look as though they are sitting very firmly on their mounts. These Mehara camels not only have great endurance on a trek, but also can gallop as fast as a racehorse. I was assured that they could go the equivalent of fifty miles per hour, but the *chamelier*, or camel boy, had a dreamy look in his eyes, and I have an idea that this was a desert fisherman's story. A camel's life cycle is roughly that of a horse. They start their training when they are about four years old and live for about twenty years.

After a tour around we arrived back on the outskirts of the village where we made a friendly connaissance with a troop of eight camels resting there. All of them had one knee tied, except the leader who had to rest in prayer all the time with both knees hobbled.

The clear sun of this morning had eaten all the soft and varied colours of the day before, but it left me with a memory of two completely different desert days. While returning by the football ground, where from my superior position I could see over the wall and watch the bare-footed Arab boys attacking a football, I was startled by a cry of '*Attention*' from my *chamelier*. Some of the Arab boys were climbing through a drain to get a better view of this apparition on a camel with the not so remote hope of scaring my active pure-bred steed, for he was quick on his feet and could shy like a horse. Luckily for me the camel was more interested in the sound of an aircraft revving on the distant airfield. In order to distract his attention from this interruption of the desert silence, I caressed his hump with my heels. I do not know whether he liked this, but there seemed to be no harm in trying!

When we got back to the hotel, the *chamelier* again hissed at the Mehara and with a low noise of resentment and a grunt it heaved itself down on to its knees and then collapsed behind. I climbed out of the high cross piece in front and wooden back of the *rehalla*, and arrived safely '*à terre.*' The camel got up again but the *chamelier* had forgotten to give me my shoes, tied under one of the gaily coloured rugs hanging from the *rehalla*. Instead of reaching up to unhitch them, the camel was told to lie down again while the shoes were retrieved. I was surrounded by barefooted Arabs and I felt quite self-conscious as I shuffled into my shoes.

We lunched with the crew of our plane, this time on perfectly cooked pheasant. There was certainly no need to go to Paris for food, if one could eat like a king in the desert. When we were all replete and in a good mood for our northward flight, we went to the airport where the ladies were called on board first. There were only a few passengers, so I had the choice of one hundred and twelve seats.

Once we were airborne into the clear sky, I had a bird's eye view of the vast loneliness of the desert. From the time we took off, we flew for an hour over endless sandy ridges and mountains without a sign of any kind of life.

We landed at Ghardaïa, a more prosperous oasis than El Goléa, with five towns built along a valley. I was told that the oasis kept moving farther down the ancient river bed and so each time a more modern town grew up around the spring. Thus the most ancient town was the poorest and the farthest from the essential water supply.

We changed a few of our passengers and were off again within ten minutes. From there, again we passed over ridges of sand, and desolate plains until we had flown over the oasis of Laghouat and on until we saw the inland salt lakes of *chotts*.   As it had rained recently these lakes were full of water, but in the summer they become dry, leaving just the white residue of salt.

We were now flying over mountains and hills, spotted with shrubs and stunted trees.   In this part of the country falcons were used for hunting the hare.   This popular and old-established sport had unfortunately been curtailed owing to the troubles in the north, otherwise I had been invited to spend a day or so seeing the falcons, their training and the actual hunting of the hare.   Sometime I hope I may avail myself of the kind invitation of the family of Bey Bou-Mezrag, who have all the traditions of the sport of 'La Fauconnerie' in their blood.

As a change of sport, I had been asked to go ski-ing the next day in the Kabylie Mountains not far from Algiers. Unfortunately the bandits got there first, and so we used discretion and did not go to join them.   Instead, we returned by train to Lavarande, to celebrate the Feast of the Epiphany.   During dinner, Balkacem, the Arab servant, brought in the traditional ring-shaped cake.   I cut a sliver and was surprised to find a bean in it.   There were cries from the others of, 'Why, how lucky, you are the Queen.'

Later, while I was writing, my host started drawing cartoons, and disclosed his great talent, depicting my efforts at camel riding.

I left Algiers in spring-like weather and as we flew over a sunny island, the flight sheet was passed down the plane.   It read—Position: Majorca—Destination: Paris— Weather in Paris: *Il neige*.   Sure enough, the countryside

was white when we came out of the clouds to land at
Orly. A blizzard was blowing at the airport, and I
shivered as I waited to change planes for London.

I was then told that at any moment there might be
a strike. Some planes ready to take off on the runway, had to return, as the strike was suddenly announced
and the control tower refused to let them take off.
The passengers disconsolately walked back through the
snow. After this, no one was sure if and when planes
would fly again.

I spent the next twenty-four hours phoning the airport
and thinking of the sun I had left down south. Luckily
I got back the next day and found London bathed in
sunshine. I could hardly believe that I had been away
for only a week.

The Best Camel in the World
Met Miss Pat Smythe in the Sahara
And the consequence was . . . The Camel collapsed

CHAPTER 7

Joy Without Jumping

WHEN Prince Hal and I were invited to join the team for the Madrid Horse Show in 1951, not only was it Prince Hal's first international show but it was also my first visit to Spain. I was determined to learn a little Spanish before I left and so I bought a second-hand grammar book and studied it for a week or two.

No sooner had I arrived in Spain than I was asked by some gentleman if I could speak any Spanish. I haltingly explained that I was just trying to learn a little from a book, but I had only got to the first sentences. The first sentence happened to be an example illustrating the use of 'which' and 'what'. It read, 'What are your intentions?' As quick as lightning the reply came back, '*Muy malo*'—very bad. So I stopped using my Spanish until I had learnt some more basic grammar and vocabulary.

My Spanish progressed during the two weeks of the horse show both in 1951 and 1954, but I had always longed to go to the south of Spain and to travel without the responsibility of the horses.

In the spring of 1955 I was invited to go to the Feria at Seville and stay in the Palacio de las Duenas, the famous Moorish palace and show place belonging to the Duke of Alba and home of the Duke and Duchess of Montoro. Unfortunately I could not get to Andalucia in time for the

Feria. I was jumping in Algiers and the weekly plane for Spain left on a Monday, the day of the last competition. There was no other means of transport to get to Seville and then to England in time for the Taunton Jumping Festival, so for the time being I had to abandon this chance of visiting Andalucia.

It has always been difficult to fit in any social events or holidays between shows, but last September I managed to steal away. The ground was very hard and the horses needed a short rest, so, with no special plan, I suddenly decided to explore Spain for a week.

Before I left, the horses earned their rest by jumping at shows on two consecutive days. The first show at Lambourn had an unusual class called 'The Best Family Turnout'. This was a serious event with mothers and daughters dressed in their smartest hunting kit riding horses and ponies immaculately turned out with plaited manes and tails. I was asked to join a less serious outfit of Lady Mary Rose Williams's family circus, with her daughter dressed as a fairy balancing on her pony, and Lady Mary Rose dressed as a ring master—with dashing side whiskers and a moustache, leading her show jumper Grey Skies. I was perched on Grey Skies, without a saddle and dressed in cowboy clothes, strumming the guitar. Whether the music inspired Grey Skies or the ring master dropped him on purpose I do not know, but suddenly the horse pricked his ears and with reins trailing he galloped at a large triple bar and jumped it from the wrong side. I managed to stay on by the skin of my teeth and a string of the guitar. Later that evening there was more entertainment with the cowboy clothes, an ideal outfit for a barbecue and a cabaret which followed.

The next day at Thame Show Flanagan won the open jumping and Hal helped Gloucestershire to qualify for the next round of the inter-county jumping, before they went home for their ten days' rest. I caught the first plane to Madrid and the following morning I was having my first lesson in caping. My instructor was Carmencita, daughter of the Duke and Duchess of Pinohermoso, and with classical stance and dignified expression, she showed me how to move the cape for a *Verónica*, a *media verónica* and a *larga cambiada*. Then with the *muleta* we tried to basic pass of a *natural* and a *trincherazo*, the pass used to sober unruly bulls. I wondered if I would keep my feet still and my movements graceful and at the same time if I would remember which pass to use as a huge and ferocious bull charged at me like an express train. I decided I wouldn't, so we put the capes away and I rested my aching wrists.

We then rode out to see the bulls on the range, and we each carried a long wooden pole called a *garrocha*. My arm got very tired with the weight of this pole, and I am sure that I could not have used it to ward off an angry cow, let alone have handled it to throw a bull. The old hands can gallop behind the bulls and at the right moment they touch the bull's haunches with the *garrocha* which makes it lose its balance and fall. A novice at the job can easily break his arm or even fall off in his effort to '*derribar los mansos*' as it is called, but the smallest man who knows the timing and knack can put the largest bull off its feet.

I thought that this was not quite in my line either, so I returned to the bull ring for the quieter occupation of riding a high school horse. This perfectly schooled chestnut gelding was called Falcon, and he knew as much about bulls and bullfighting as his trainer and master, the Duke. They had fought bulls together all over Spain, and I have rarely seen or ridden such a beautiful and intelligent horse. He was as light as a feather on his feet, and gaily and gracefully performed any movement one wished, from a Spanish walk, like the goose-step, to a pirouette with either foreleg held out in front of him. I merely had to think of the movements and he divined my thoughts.

Early the next morning we came out of the yards and climbed up on the high surrounding wall. Six of the four-year-old '*toros bravos*' were being brought in from the freedom of their pasture as they had been sold for a big *corrida* in the north of Spain. The mists were rising from the Guadarrama Mountains, showing the dark outline of the Cruz de los Caidos, the great cross built in memory of the victims of the Civil War. Following the ridge of the hills to the south, I could see the solid grey granite of the Escorial, reigning in severe dignity over the village clustered at its feet. This massive palace has sheltered monks and kings, and still inspires awe in those who see it rising above the plain, looking even more sombre in the shadow of the mountains.

Below the Escorial lay another bull breeding farm or *finca*, where much of *Richard III* had been filmed, with gipsies travelling miles to this spot in the hopes that some of their horses would be hired for the scenes.

At that moment I saw a cloud of dust approaching, with three *vaqueros*, cattlemen, carrying their *garrochas*, galloping behind. Out of the dust appeared the tame black and white steers used for bringing in the bulls, and

Princess Margaret talking to Prince Hal

Noel Whitcomb introduces mc to Danny Kaye

Brigadoon

Brigadoon's first jump

Further lessons

At home, jumping for joy

Flanagan

Prince Hal

among them were the six sleek and fit, fighting bulls. The *vaqueros* were not quite close enough and one bull outstripped the others and broke away from the long funnel of wire fence that led to the gates of the bull yard.

The *vaqueros* doubled back and got the steers and bulls together again. The steers knew the way into the yard and they were driven at a thundering gallop down through the gates. It was a spectacular sight and after seeing this I felt a deep respect for the men who run before the bulls through the streets of Pamplona at the festival of San Firmin, as is the custom for the '*encierro*', or collecting of the bulls.

The bulls became quiet with the calming influence of the steers and we were able to inspect them from the safety of our wall. They looked magnificent as they had been fed on corn and the fat of the land for all their lives.

I was then taken to see another country place away in the mountains, where the breeding cows were kept and pastured during the summer months. We drove over a rough track, right out of sight of any human habitation or road until we arrived at the bungalow and stables used by the family when they stayed there. It was furnished simply and practically inside, with almost the only decoration on the walls being the wooden crucifixes above the beds and one or two photos of famous bulls that had been bred there. Looking down the lovely valley flanked with hills of speckly green, I felt the peace and beauty of this lovely and tranquil place.

As a contrast, we had supper in Madrid, at an old *bodega* full of *flamenco* song and guitars. The friends gathered were not tourists and the singing and playing was for their genuine enjoyment. While I was watching

I left the hotel and went to see the Murillo and Zurbarán pictures in the lovely and enormous Gothic cathedral. It was at the time of high mass and I heard the singing and the wonderful tones of the organ. The organist played a Bach fugue with perfect interpretation in this rich setting and an incomparable contrast to the rattle of the early morning. Incidentally, at the same time my brother was being ordained priest at Chelmsford, and apart from being present with him there, the atmosphere of the cathedral and its beauty were ideally conducive to thought and prayer.

After this I wandered through the Court of Orange Trees, and as I looked up at the great bell tower of the cathedral called Giralda, I received an eyeful of chipped stone. The court of the old mosque was being repaired, and the workmen did not worry who received their chippings! I found that it was better to climb up the Giralda above the 'reparations' and scaffolding. From the top of the tower, which had been the minaret of the old mosque and the masterpiece of Jebir the Moor, I surveyed Seville with its Moorish houses and palaces, narrow streets and bull ring and away across the Guadalquivir river to Triana, the gipsy quarter, on the other bank. Below me were horse and mule carriages looking like leisurely moving ants, as they took their passengers around the squares and down the Paseo de las Delicias to the Parque de Maria Luisa. In the park one could take a siesta sitting beneath the palms and orange trees, surrounded by roses, camellias and tall acacias.

In the afternoon, I wanted to get to Jerez de la Frontera, and I imagined that a train would be the quickest means of transport. The train left at 3.30 p.m. and as we did not start lunch until after 3 o'clock, we were still chewing our last mouthful as we arrived breathless at the station. We rushed on to the platform asking anxiously, 'Has the train gone? Which platform for Jerez? Quickly, please tell us.' The porters looked at me as though we were crazy. Again I said, 'Have we missed the train?' The slow reply came. 'The train is at least two hours behind time, maybe three hours. *Quien sabe*— who knows?' I then discovered that I could catch a bus two hours later and still arrive in Jerez before the train.

The four-hour bus journey is worth recording and the passengers were very different from those one would meet on a London to Cheltenham run. In the first place our tickets were numbered and my seat was right behind the driver. On one side I had a gipsy woman nursing a baby and on the other side a nun, with large and protruding wings to her headdress. Most of the passengers were workmen with one or two very tough and swarthy characters among them. There were no other girls travelling unaccompanied and I could not very well look as though I belonged to either of my next-door neighbours.

When all the seats had been taken, and then the passage seats pulled down to fill the bus solidly, there were still two more people to get in. One man, a friend of the driver, was put in the middle seat of the three across the front of the bus, with the driver on his left and the last passenger, an old gipsy woman of eighty-five, on his right. This must have been one of the first bus rides for the 'granny' and she cackled with delight as we bounced and rattled along over the potholes at breakneck speed,

We sat round a little table under the pine trees at the edge of the wood, and while we were talking, gipsies appeared out of the woods and greeted Señor Domecq. Before we had been there ten minutes, there were at least six additions to our table. More sherry was opened and the talk was of old times and past happenings in the locality.

As the table behind us accumulated the empty sherry bottles so the atmosphere mellowed and the guitars were produced. In this home of *flamenco* I heard the original folk songs of Cadiz and Jerez, sung by the gipsies born and bred with this music in their blood. We stayed the whole night through, watching whenever one of the company was inspired to dance on the pine needles. The guitarist asked me what I would like to hear. I requested some of the lovely and melodious *malaguenas* and *soleares*, particular to that district. As he started to play, he dedicated his song to me in flowing and eloquent Spanish. The warm night air was slowly dissolved by the fresh mists of morning and the high-pitched whine of mosquitoes was replaced by the early birdsong. I returned to the hotel to change in readiness for my tour around the *finca*, arranged at an early hour that morning.

We travelled the rough roads in a jeep, leaping the potholes and occasionally veering over at a dangerous angle as we took to the fields to avoid an even worse piece of track. Although there were few villages on the road, we passed fields of cotton full of woman and children bent low as they picked, their heads covered with a cloth to protect them from the sun. We drove through a high gate in the wire fence and across a large and hilly field to see the magnificent fighting bulls. We admired from a distance before returning to the converted monastery and stockyards.

Inside the charming house, with low and rounded construction in the Roman style, it was cool and restful to the eyes. One side of the house looked out over a valley to the orchards and groves of olives and orange trees beyond. Along the passage through the house, the original monks' cells had been converted into little bedrooms and sitting rooms for the various members of the family. The far end of the house opened on to a private bull ring, where friends could come and watch the testing of the stock bred on the *finca*. The whole farm was run on a large and efficient scale, with a great deal of machinery. The tractors could fill up from a large tank of gas oil. The owner had found it more practical to keep this tank and instal an expensive filter to extract the high water content from the fuel.

When I got back to Jerez, I was shown round the *bodega* of the Domecqs. I had never realized the long history behind the making of the great sherries and brandies, but I soon learned that it needs a lifetime of experience to know all the necessary blends and types of grapes in order to produce the varieties of wine required. I tasted a dark and bitter wine that was two hundred years old, and different sherries from huge casks, often named after famous people from Napoleon to Sir Winston Churchill.

That afternoon we drove across dirt roads through the vineyards that produce this unique wine, and past the castle tower that is now portrayed on the bottles that bear the label of Pedro Domecq. We raised clouds of white, penetrating dust as we travelled farther along policeman was so occupied with. All I could see were signs like a game of noughts and crosses. Later I told my host what I had seen, and he, unsurprised, told me that few of the local boys could write.

Although some Spaniards do not always take pride in literary knowledge, often there is a great satisfaction in the work they do achieve. I saw a bricklayer building a house that grew from hour to hour. His chief delight was that the labourers were worn out by the speed that he demanded in supplying loads of bricks. With easy expertness he was proud to lay at least four thousand bricks a day—an interesting example for some of our unions!

The only other time I had two unexpected days in Spain happened on the way back from Algiers. Three of us had flown from Toulouse and from there, met by Jacquie, the wife of Pierrot Jonquères d'Oriola, we had driven back together to their home near Perpignan. Jonquères and Paco Goyoaga were going on to Nice for the International Horse Show later that week but in the meantime he had to get things arranged at home before he left. Apart from his vineyards and farm, there was other work in progress, with part of the farm house being rebuilt to convert it into a suitable house for himself and his wife.

That evening, when everyone was very busy, Paco and I found a two-horse-power Citroen in one of the farm buildings and realizing that all the family had their hands full and that we could be of no help, we decided to go to Spain.

Once we had got the car started and found that it worked, we set off immediately. We passed through vineyards with their regiments of vines standing in neat rows at attention, awaiting the command of Summer to produce their fruit in time for the grape harvest. Bullocks, blocking our way with laden carts, would take their time as they pensively drew aside, only to be engulfed in the wake of white dust raised by our car.

We headed south for the Pyrenees. Chugging along at a steady twenty miles per hour, our average decreased as the mountains rose before us. With much gear usage, patience and a fair trail of oil on the road, we managed to make the frontier post at La Jonquera.

Full of confidence and with only thought of the easy descent ahead, our buoyant spirits were quickly deflated by a Spanish customs official. He wanted to see the car's papers. Of course, the car having being used on the Jonquères' farm for all of its tough life, did not have any papers. What was the engine number? Nobody knew, and the entire frontier guard pulled the car to pieces before the number was found somewhere in the boot tucked behind the back axle. Was the owner driving? No, the car belonged to a Frenchman and the driver was a Spaniard with an English passenger. 'Impossible!' The official shook his head and took my passport, looking at the first visa that had been issued for my visit in 1951. He waved his arms and said emphatically that it was absolutely impossible for a Spaniard driving someone else's French car with no papers, and carrying an English girl with an unpronounceable name in Spanish to go across the frontier to Spain.

We were determined not to admit defeat, so after careful looking up of rules and regulations it was found that a girl could drive a foreign car across the frontier without honour dressed in their Arlesian costume, brightly coloured with brocaded skirts, and lace *chapelles* round their necks. Then came the bride's father, riding a white horse of the Camargue, with the bride herself sitting behind him on the horse's croup. She looked ravishingly charming with her flowing white dress, and lace top, with a little lace *coiffe* like two butterfly's wings on her head. Behind them came the Guardians, the horsemen of the Camargue that look after the fighting bulls bred on the marshes. These eighteen men had ridden their little grey horses many miles, from their homes on the Camargue to Arles, the night before. None of the horses had shoes, and they certainly did not know the meaning of a stable or clippers. The men were dressed in their usual costume, with broad-brimmed hats, short jackets, bow tie, and trousers tight fitting to the knee with bell bottoms. They all carried the tridents they use when working with the bulls. These tridents are like a Spanish *pica*, except that the long wooden lance has a small three-pronged steel end. Each trident had a white ribbon on it, except for those carrying the banners embroidered with the arms of each of the families due to be married.

At the door of the chapel the bride was lifted down from her father's horse and six tiny bridesmaids came to meet her. Each child carried a little bouquet of cornflowers, and their long white dresses were decked with cornflowers around the skirt and chains of blue flowers crowning their heads. The procession then walked up to the chapel under the arch of tridents held by the eighteen horsemen. They were led by the pipers, maids of honour and the bridesmaids, with the bride on her father's arm, followed by the bridegroom and the family.

Flanagan

Hal after winning
the *Daily Mail* Cup

Flanagan at the trot—   —and at the canter

TRAINING AT THE WINDSOR FOREST STUD

Myself on Flanagan, Peter Robeson on Craven A, and our trainer, Lt.-Col. Talbot-Ponsonby

Prince Hal at Badminton

Training rounds at Badminton
on Flanagan and Scorchin'

Only a few of the many people there could fit into the chapel to hear the service, which was taken by the Archbishop of Avignon, who had also performed the same ceremony for the bride's father. During the service, two of the maids of honour came forward and veiled the bride and then unveiled her as the vows were made. When the ceremony was over, the married couple came out from the chapel under a double arch of swords held by some of the officers of the bridegroom's regiment of the Deuxiéme Regiment Etranger de Cavalerie, surmounted by the tridents of the Guardians.

The horsemen had to draw back and allow everyone to file past and congratulate the married couple and family. The cars of the guests drove away to La Cavalerie, the family house where the reception was to be held. Eventually the bride and bridegroom were taken in a grey *vedette* Ford, surrounded by the Guardian horsemen and clouds of dust. After the last good-byes had been said, the Comte himself leapt on to his horse and galloped after them taking a short cut across the fields and ditches.

At the house about three hundred guests sat down to the wedding breakfast. If there had been no mistral the reception could have been outside, but alas, the wind was '*épouvantable*'.

The delicious *vin rosé* that accompanied the meal was the wine of the estate. It also helped to wash down the dust blown up by the wind, that had collected in people's throats. This was followed, according to the stage of the meal, by red wine, and then champagne. By about four p.m. the guests were ready for the excellent and witty speeches from the bride's grandfather, the Marquis de Roux, and the bridegroom's brother. The leader of the

Camargue use these tough ponies for riding over the marshes in their work with the cattle.

There is a fascination in this land although the lovely beaches are full of mosquitoes and the fierce mistral wind is nearly always blowing. The men who live there are poor but happy, and they bless the two plagues of wind and insects, that keep their country from being besieged by tourists.

I had already stayed in the ancient and ruined town of Les Baux, built on the weird and unearthly heights of the Alpilles Mountains rising jaggedly out of the plains to the north of Arles and Beaucaire. All Provence is full of ancient tradition and even the language has roots older than Latin. The bargemen on this part of the Rhône use the terms *Royaume* and *Empire* for starboard and port, depending on their journey upstream or downstream. This is a survival from the time when the Rhône was the boundary between the Kingdom of France and the Holy Roman Empire, with Beaucaire on the 'Kingdom' bank and Tarascon on the 'Empire' side of the river.

On the way down the river, one passes through the magnificent old Roman cities of Valence, Montelimar, now famed for nougat, Orange with its great Roman theatre, and Avignon the walled city and home of the Popes during the 'Babylonish Captivity' of the fourteenth century.

Then there is Tarascon with its towers and castles, and the Roman buildings of Arles and Nîmes, both with their arenas that are still able to seat twenty thousand spectators to-day. Those arenas must have seen many changes, varying from gladiators and lions and Christian martyrs, to bull fights.

This fascinating country is divided into three provinces,

with Languedoc to the west of the Rhône, Provence to the east of the Rhône and the Camargue between the two mouths of the river.

Not long ago, a friend who was staying with me, a French girl called Brigitte, suddenly decided to join me on a visit to a ceremony in Aix-en-Provence. We did a marathon drive, from Paris to the south and during the week-end we visited my friends the Comte and Comtesse de Roux, where I had stayed the year before, for the wedding of their daughter, Irène.

By now, kind people had assured me that my French was without an accent, although I knew my limitations and lack of grammatical background and vocabulary. Even the first assurance was shattered when I telephoned these good friends whom I had not seen for some time. I had found myself within eighty kilometres of their estate and so rang up to see if we could drive over to visit the family. When the phone was answered my greeting was cut short by 'Vous exagérez trop'. I could not think what was meant by this or why I was exaggerating too much, but in the next moment I was given a pressing invitation to come over for dinner that night. Later I found out that it was thought that I was a French friend who had been to England, and used to ring up assuming an English accent! So my English accent was even more exaggerated!

On the way to the Camargue, Brigitte and I stopped for lunch at the old fishing port of Martigues. It is between the sea and the great fresh water lake of the Etang de Berre. The water ways and canals have given it the nickname of the Venice of France, but really it is a genuine fisherman's village, happily not as yet geared for before the relics are returned to the Church for another year. This great event is accompanied by a huge horse fair, with bull fights, dances and carousels.

The chapel of Saint Sarah, which is in the crypt of the church, has served in ancient times as the altar of Cybele, Diana of Ephesus, and Mithras.

We finished the evening in a *cabane* of one of the Guardians. Here we heard stories of the people who had come to make films with this wild but picturesque country as a background. The Guardians themselves loved taking part in scenes that needed men on horseback, or the bulls bred and raised on the marshes. Then a project was started to make a film of the Guardians and their work.

They agreed to help, provided that it was an authentic account of their lives. However, when the script was produced, the story was not only completely inaccurate about all that they did, but also brought in cattle thieves and dishonest Guardians that had never existed. The producer had wanted sensation and effect and so had used his own imagination to conjure up his story. He would have done better to have used the Guardian's real adventures, which occur all the time.

Looking after fighting bulls is dangerous enough in itself, but the great sport of Provence is the 'Courses de Cocardes'. A bull is let into the ring and the young men try to capture the *cocarde* or rosette that is fastened between its horns. The more dangerous the bull, the higher price in francs is placed on the *cocarde*. With a renowned bull, that has already killed several people, the *cocarde* may be worth as much as £100, but a life is risked each time a man attempts to snatch the prize.

In the Spanish and Portuguese bull-fighting, each bull

has one fight in its life, which lasts for only twenty minutes. During this short time the bull learns about his enemy, the man holding the cape, and becomes more dangerous and cunning all through the fight. The moment before he is killed, he is at his most dangerous because he may have learnt to look at the man instead of following the red cloth in his hand. It is at this 'moment of truth' that most matadors get gored or killed, when they have to pass right over the horn in the action of killing the bull.

In the 'Courses de Cocardes', the bull is used for any number of fights and is never killed. The breeder of a renowned bull gets a very high price for hiring him to the villages for their fights. The more times the bull comes into contact with men, the more cunning he learns with the old stagers becoming very dangerous indeed.

I was shown the head of a bull mounted on the wall of the cabane. The Guardian who had bred him, told me proudly, 'This horn', pointing to the right one, 'has killed nine people. A great bull famous in the history of the Camargue.' Apparently he had always hooked with his right horn when he wished to kill his assailant, and he had usually achieved his aim. A tough way of earning money and getting one's sport.

It was no wonder that the Guardians were horrified by the film producer's idea of life in the Camargue. He refused to change his script to a more accurate and equally exciting story, so the Guardians naturally declined to be filmed in these roles, and give a false impression of their life to the public. This was a great decision, made for their belief in Truth, for money is hard to come by in their exacting work, and they were giving up the film wages that would have helped them combat the poverty of the winter months.

We returned to the *mas*, as the estates are called in this part, for an excellent dinner of home-grown rice and home-produced wine. During dinner we heard another story. One day a visitor, who had come to stay with the Comte de Roux, especially wanted to see the Camargue on horseback. In this he showed good sense, for it is the only way to get to know this country, which has few roads or ways for motor transport.

The Count was very busy at the time with the rice harvest, but kindly offered to lend the visitor his best horse. This white cowpony had been bred on the Camargue and knew the land and the way of the bulls from his training and instinct. Riding over the marshes, one finds much of the land is under water, with shallow pools and creeks, and sandy ridges covered with white layers of salt. It is usually safe to splash one's way through the water, but there are a few boggy places. The ponies know when the ground is not safe and refuse to go near a bog. So when the visitor mounted for his ride, the Count warned him, 'If the pony stops suddenly, do not push him, for there may be a bog, and you can always ride around the dangerous places'.

The visitor went off for his ride and the Count went to see how the harvest was progressing on his three farms. It was dark by the time the Count arrived home for dinner, after a long and tiring day in the rice fields. 'What have you done with your friend?' he was asked by his wife. He was horrified. '*Zut alors!* Isn't he back yet and he's on my best horse!'

A search party was organized, and the men, tired

from their day's work, braved the mistral wind to catch their horses, saddle them and ride off in the hope of finding the visitor. They did not have far to look, for there he was sitting on the horse in the middle of a field. He had been there since the early afternoon, when the horse had stopped, realizing that the rider on its back was a novice. The visitor was afraid to push it on after the warning of bogs and so had waited in the dry field until night time for his rescuers. No doubt he would have spent the night there as well, unless the horse had kindly decided to take him home!

Like many things done on the spur of the moment, our journey worked out perfectly although nothing had been planned beforehand. During the week-end we saw Provence and the Côte d'Azur, completely free from tourists and in a different dress from its usual summer costume. The terrible winter had left the palm and olive trees grey and gaunt. Farmers did not know if their vines were still alive or if the plants would show signs of life again when spring eventually came. I met a friend of over eighty years old who wandered round his garden snapping off dead twigs and saying pathetically, 'Never before in my life have these trees been killed by the cold. It is unbelievable that this should happen in the South of France.'

On our journey we were able to stop our little car at any interesting place, and while we were driving we kept each other awake by singing French and Spanish songs and also with serious discussions. Brigitte had been living near Caen in Normandy at the time of the Allied landings there on D-Day in June 1944. She was only a child, but the family had survived on the battlefront living in the woods and surrounded by death and destruction.

She had been left with the impression that death was a bitter and lonely end, whereas although I feel one should live in preparation for death, it cannot be lonely if life has led to its proper goal. I felt how little I know of the sufferings of people who have lost everything in an invaded country. Not only every possession, but losing children and parents, friends and relations, and to find themselves without security in a country taken by unscrupulous conquerors. This terrible thought made me even more grateful for my secure upbringing and good fortune of my home, nationality and country.

I had to catch a plane from Paris on the Tuesday morning, and after a reception at the Mairie with speeches and a welcome from the Mayor himself, Brigitte and I did not leave Aix-en-Provence until Monday afternoon. We had promised ourselves an unhurried drive back to Paris, so that we could recuperate from our hectic and tiring week-end. Imagine our pleasure and surprise when Uffa Fox, the sailing and boat-designing expert, blew in from out of the blue on a breeze of laughter, with sailing friends *en route* for some races in Cannes. Of course this unexpected reunion called for a celebration lunch and eventually we sailed away in our car at tea time.

We drove northwards relentlessly through the rainy evening until we had passed the remaining snow drifts on the edge of the Massif Central. At 2.30 in the morning we could keep awake no longer, and we found a room at our second attempt, in a hotel in Bourges.

At 6.30 in the morning the proprietor banged on our

door and told us the hot coffee was outside. There was not even a whisper of a reply from either of us. A quarter of an hour later a grieved French voice told us the coffee was now cold and still outside the door.

Still silent, we got up and dressed and only after a little cold coffee could we speak enough to ask for the bill. When we went outside the sun was shining and we found that we felt less tired now that we had achieved the effort of getting up. We went to the lovely Cathedral of Bourges to say our morning prayers and then drove on north to Paris through the sunlit country of the Loire, looking so different from the previous days of grey skies.

We arrived at the airport one minute ahead of schedule. I wished Brigitte *au revoir*, flew to England and was riding Flanagan in his Olympic training at Ascot by 2 p.m. that afternoon.

SECOND CONVERSATION PIECE

Two point-to-point horses are overheard in the horse box discussing the days racing.

1ST HORSE: How are your tendons feeling?

2ND HORSE: I've an idea that they're fresher than my jockey's biceps—because I really felt like pulling to-day.

1ST: Did you hear my owner trying to get a tip on your rider's chances?

2ND: A tip from him was it, begorra! Why he has to hire a man to call his chickens in, because if he told them that it was bedtime they wouldn't believe him!

1ST: Well, he wasn't shivering in the paddock before the race like most of the green jockeys that are put up on me.

2ND: No, mine was getting some dutch courage judging by the way he staggered into the paddock just as the bell was ringing for 'jockeys up'.

1ST: I can't stick all that walking round the paddock with punters hanging over the rails making rude remarks about the way my head is left unclipped—let them try to shave me!

2ND: Well I must say that I kicked up a shindy to-day, with that cold wind under my tail. My hindquarters felt so bouncey in the paddock that no one could get near enough to tighten my girth.

1ST: I thought you were going round the course the wrong way when your jockey couldn't pull you up after cantering down to the start.

2ND: I nearly did because anyway he usually sits back, holding on to the buckle of the reins before the first fence even comes over the horizon.

1ST: Don't mention the first fence, I didn't see it in the scrum and just found myself the other side luckily still on my feet. I never got properly away at the start as I had that surly old kicker next to me and none of us would go near him to line up. We played up so much before we were off that it gave the Starter a job as bad as herding mice at a cross roads! You were O.K. because you were kept well away from us, and anyway you nipped off to a good start almost before the flag was dropped.

2ND: (*hastily*) Did you see me on my nose after the drop fence? I don't know how my jockey didn't fall off but he held on with his hands under my chin and his shoulders over my eyes and ears. I just staggered up and galloped on blindfold until he worked himself back down my neck to the saddle.

1ST: My dear chap, I was beside you and while your jockey was doing a handstand on your head, my rider asked him if he was all right. I hope you didn't hear his reply and remarks about your jumping! I was laughing so much that I forgot to take off at the open ditch and hit it at the roots.

2ND: I wondered why there was such a big hole in the fence and I nearly fell there the second time round because I tried to jump through the gap.

1ST: We both seem to have had an exciting race. I wonder you were still pulling so hard at the finish.

2ND: Oh, I like to lean on my jockey, that's why I'm never put in a ladies' race because they can't hold me.

1ST: You miss a lot of fun, we have a rare old time and.

[195]

my goodness, some of them make remarks not suitable for a well bred horse's ears! I'll tell you another thing. Once I had a new girl jockey put on me and I guessed by her determined riding that I had to win. However, as we came over the last fence, that good horse Winalot came alongside me, full of running and ridden by some mug. My rider guessed that I was outclassed and knocked the whip out of the other girl's hand, as Winalot passed me! Of course he's a lazy horse and his girl didn't know how to use her legs, so I just got up and beat him by a whisker.

2ND: That's nothing to the way my rider made me jump a good friend into the wing the other day.

1ST: I know, I can bring down nearly any rival by making them take off too far from a fence.

2ND: Really, aren't we a crooked lot, you'll be saying you give your jockey stimulants soon.

1ST: What, and then cut the telephone wires when I've got my oats on him!

2ND: Talking of oats, I feel too excited to eat after that finish. Every time I think of it I break out in a sweat.

1ST: You'll be popular when your groom takes off your rugs and finds you in a lather. You want to relax and think about dull things like counting show jumpers going over fences.

Flanagan over the White City water

Commander Collins handing me the Olympic Torch

Jump for joy, with the cold wind under Flanagan's tail

Flanagan winning the Grand Military Prize at Lucerne

Prince Hal at Lucerne winning the Prix du Pilate

Prince Hal in the Puissance at Stockholm

Two water jumps; training and the real thing

CHAPTER 8

Brigadoon

BRIGADOON is a young horse that has not yet hit the headlines and may never do so. In the story of his training, however, I can show some of the background work that any young show jumper needs.

In the spring of 1954 I received a letter which said that a young horse was for sale. He was unbroken but might become a likely jumper. The owners did not ride and therefore wished to sell him before he became too big and strong. I often get letters from people who want to get rid of youngsters, but it is usually not an economic proposition for me to buy an unbroken horse.

A great deal of time has to be spent on the 'breaking in'. First there is the general handling of the animal to get it used to people, then the gradual introduction to the saddle and bridle. During this stage the young horse is 'mouthed', teaching it how to accept the bit in its mouth and to get used to a saddle and the weight of the rider on its back. Then it must learn to adjust its own weight and balance to allow for the rider. After this, the horse is given schooling and training to make it supple and obedient.

In fact it is not ready to jump its first obstacle until months after it is first mounted. Of course, some people who have not the time or patience to go through the gradual stages of training, try for quick results. A

o   [197]

for her turn.   Horses are sensitive and they take in all that they see is happening to their friends, and they may be suspicious of a fence that has given trouble to a companion.

We then went to Dublin.   Prince Hal won a competition and with the combined results of the two horses, I had some prize money in my pocket to merit looking at some young horses.

On the day after Hal's win, I found the letter about Brigadoon, and borrowed a car to drive over the Wicklow Mountains to remote and beautiful Britters Bay. When I arrived at the charming whitewashed farmhouse, the owners of Brigadoon greeted me and took me out to the buildings, where the horse was in captivity.   A door was unbarred and a white face shot out, hardly tolerant enough for the formalities of putting on a headcollar and lunging line, which was attached somehow or other as this rampaging youngster walked all over us.

At length, he was secured and the door unbolted, whereupon he leapt forth with wide-spread nostrils to view the shimmering sea, which reflected the greeny mauve mountains dotted with the little white crofts forlornly clinging to their steep sides.

One important characteristic needed in a show jumper is a calm temperament and here was this horse with his wild thoughts and excited gaze into the distance, hardly noticing our existence right beside him.   To him, people were immaterial, unless they helped to fulfil his wish for freedom.   He obviously had character, and he was good-looking, so after he had trotted and pranced around, his lumps and bumps were questioned and passed off as merely a result of too good feeding, and too much freedom for enjoying himself.

So within a short time, the three-year-old became mine and I returned to the Dublin Spring Show to set about trying to win some more competitions with Hal and Tosca, not only to cover his cost price but also to get something towards the cost of his keep before he himself would be old enough to start jumping.

This last problem was taken off my hands by very kind friends, Mr. and Mrs. Claude Odlam, who have the mill house near Naas. Brigadoon was kept there on excellent grazing until he was ready to be shipped over to England.

He arrived early the next spring and I was thrilled to see how he had grown and developed. We turned him out on some banks near home with another chestnut thoroughbred that I had been hunting, called Cornfield. These two become great friends and were a joy to see when playing together. Both horses are very handsome and 'breedy', and both have a broad white blaze down their faces. Brigadoon has four white socks, which show up well against his brown colouring, and Cornfield has two socks. Whenever we came to feed them, they would show off in front of us and prance around with feet hardly touching the ground, seemingly dancing on air. With tails held straight out behind them like flags at the stern of a ship, and heads held proudly aloft, they would open their nostrils and send trumpeting snorts echoing around the valley.

After a buck and a kick and a gallop around, they would finish their play and come up to us, puffing from their exertions. During the summer they both put on muscle with the good food and grass, and they grew fit from playing on the hillside. It was a very dry summer and the ground became harder until it was like concrete.

standing still. I praised him for his good behaviour while I was mounting and we started work again. The next time he felt the cold under his tail, and the hot blood coursing through his veins, I was ready for him and expressed my immediate disapproval of his naughtiness. By the end of the morning he was behaving very well and had realized that athletic rodeo displays were not included in 'school hours'.

So his training progressed, although it was not very concentrated work, owing to my going away to jump at Geneva, to ride camels in Algeria and to jump again in Brussels. Then he had time to relax in the freedom of the fields for a few hours each day, before coming back to his work with even more interest.

By the spring I was training for the Olympic Games at Ascot. We had brought up Flanagan from Miserden for this training programme, and as I had plenty of time to work other horses Brigadoon came up for intermittent weeks, to get experience in new stables and grounds and continue with his training.

Before being taken to Ascot he went to his first horse show as a companion to Prince Hal. On Easter Monday Hal was having his first outing since the indoor shows at the beginning of March and his triumphant time in Brussels. I took him to a liitle show at Wapley in the Berkeley Vale, not far from the village of Cromhall where my mother had been born and brought up.

Brigadoon came along in the horse box with Hal, so that he could get his first experience of a crowd and the many strange horses. He was astounded at his surroundings when we arrived, so I rode him around and gave him some schooling work, to show him that there was nothing too unusual about this day away from home. He was very good and accepted these new sights and sounds with intelligent interest. His eyes were popping out on stalks most of the time, but he still obeyed me although he shouted out an exuberant whinny each time he saw a chestnut horse, thinking that it was Hal. After an hour or two, Brigadoon was returned to the box and Prince Hal came out to jump immaculately in the open class.

The next day they both came to Ascot with me. Brigadoon was astonished at the lovely Royal yard where he was stabled, but his one idea was to get out of his palatial box and on to the green lawn in the middle. He was so excited with the sight of other horses, most of them Olympic possibles and show-jumping stars, that he could not tear himself away from the door. He hardly ate for days, occasionally dashing to his haynet and snatching a mouthful of hay before rushing back to the door to chew it, while wisps of hay dropped from the corners of his mouth on to the cleanly swept path outside the boxes!

Every time other horses were taken in or out of the yard, we would have to shut the top of his door, because in his excitement we were afraid that he would try to jump out. Paul despaired of his settling down, and meantime he was losing weight from not eating. In spite of this his work could not have been better, and he learnt to trot over poles, lowered to a few inches off the ground from the Olympic heights of the other horses.

At first he would forget that his hind legs had to follow his fore legs over the poles, but after making a tremendous effort in front and then treading on the poles behind, he gradually learnt the right idea. Then he started picking up each hind leg carefully as he trotted over the poles.

eyes to the difference between our wartime gymkhanas and my first sight of the post-war foreign shows. The fences were much more interesting than the usual six or seven fences one had to jump in the local shows at home. There were banks and ditches to jump as well as gay flowers around, beside and sometimes even on top of the fences. Goldfish swam among the water lilies in the little water jumps, and occasionally a rider joined the goldfish if a horse stopped suddenly. Finality got into most trouble with the doubles and trebles and combinations of fences placed with only one or two strides between them. I did not push her enough when the distances allowed for a big stride between, and probably did not ride quietly enough when there was only sufficient room for a very little stride. Still, we gained experience the hard way, and I learnt to my cost once or twice that the ground was not soft in Belgium!

For jumping in big competitions a horse must be supple like an athlete. A lot of practice is needed, for jumping over doubles, to get the horse used to making two jumping efforts with only one stride between. A grid of poles placed about ten to fifteen feet apart, depending on the size of the pony's or horse's stride, makes the horse bend its back well. In this exercise there is not enough room to take a stride between the jumps so the horse has to use all its muscles for each jumping effort.

A little free jumping in a lane may help a horse to judge its own distances and think for itself, but sometimes too much of this tends to make it very independent and not trust in the rider's judgment. The jumps must not be high when the horse is jumping free without the rider's persuasion and help, as it might hurt itself and lose confidence. Another good mounted exercise is to ride over small, wide fences placed about twenty-five feet apart. They should be jumped quietly so that the horse can drop its head to see the width of each fence.

There is an important point when turning a corner in a speed competition. If one wants to turn left the horse, must bring its head round to the left as one is turning. Then he can see the next fence while he is still on the turn and so know what to expect and begin making arrangements to meet it correctly. When a loose horse is galloping round a field he usually turns with his shoulder leading and his head turned away from the direction of the turn. In order to teach a horse to look the way he is turning, I ride around in a circle, making him look into the centre of the circle and bend his back round my inside leg. Every horse needs this suppleness of the back which is the foundation of all training.

Brigadoon is learning all these basic lessons before he can start his show jumping career. At the end of this preliminary training he started to show signs of soreness in his legs. Nature's cure for any strain on a horse's leg, is to develop little bony enlargements called 'splints' which support the weak place. Before these splints harden, they cause discomfort and pain, and the horse must be rested until he is going soundly and freely again.

A 'splint' is Nature's response to the breakdown of the fibrous union between small bones of the legs which have become displaced through jarring on hard ground. When formed, this bone weld is stronger than the original attachment.

The patience and time needed in producing a jumper is

as an unbroken four-year-old. It was only by Flanagan's own arrangement that he was bought at all. When Brigadier Bolton arrived at the farm where he was going to look at some young horses, he saw Flanagan in with the bunch of thoroughbreds grazing in the field. Although he was a more solid make and shape than his elegantly bred friends, Flanagan galloped about with the best of them.

The farmer was asked about the history of this chestnut. 'Ah sure, he just comes and goes' came the answer. It turned out that Flanagan had been bred by a poor crofter some distance away, and when the horse was lonely or hungry, he just jumped his way to better grazing or the companionship of the young thoroughbreds, before returning again to his proper home. Obviously he enjoyed jumping and had character, so he was the first choice of the day. After his owner had been found and the necessary bargain struck, the elusive horse that 'sometimes is here and sometimes is not' changed hands and came to England. Because of his great character and sense of humour, the chestnut four-year-old was appropriately named after Mr. Bud Flanagan.

In the hands of Brigadier Bolton, an excellent and experienced horseman, he had been trained and brought out for combined training competitions. He competed in the Three-day event at Badminton, and later in the same year he was fourth in the horse trials at Harewood, before being sold to Mr. Hanson. The following year I rode him for the first time in the jumping events at Harewood and again at Manchester. He came to Miserden with me after this. I had a quiet idea that he might

Morning.   Flanagan can't reach the 'out' of Fence 5

OLYMPIC GAMES, 1956

Afternoon.   A wiser horse just makes it

Last fence (second round) and still game as they come

Stockholm, June 1956.   Presentation of Medals

be an Olympic possible, although it was far too soon to know if he would make an international jumper at that stage.

I worked him at home and he was entered for some of the events at Harringay. Just before the show came the tragedy of Bill Hanson's death and, apart from losing a real friend, show jumping lost a most valuable member of the team. His friends at home and abroad mourned this sad news, and, needless to say, Flanagan stayed at home during the time of Harringay.

After Flanagan had spent the winter at Miserden, he came abroad with me for the first time in the Spring of 1955. He gained much experience at Marseilles and Algiers, and then came back to England to jump faultlessly on each day of the Taunton Jumping Festival. Later in the spring he was chosen to come as my second horse to the official Paris International Show. Prince Hal jumped in the Grand Prix events and Flanagan won three of the other events, making a most spectacular debut at this show. At the White City he won two events, confirming his international form and so meriting his selection for training.

At the end of the year, after the Harringay Show, Flanagan was roughed off and his winter coat allowed to grow. He had his shoes taken off, and steel tips put on to protect his toes, giving his feet a chance to broaden and grow. We turned him out with Tosca to get a proper rest and change of surroundings after his busy year and first full season.

When we brought him up in January, he looked like a teddy bear, but under all the woolly coat were rolls of hard fat. Even then, he was very fit as he had been turned training. Flanagan was already very fit and looking well. Although some people remarked that he looked 'as fat as a pig', it was soon proved that he was really as hard as iron!

The horses were luxuriously stabled in the lovely boxes of the Windsor Forest Stud and we worked in a field there, by the gracious permission of Her Majesty the Queen.

The riders who had been chosen for this training were Lt. Col. Harry Llewellyn, Wilfred White and Lt. Col. Duggie Stewart, all the team from the last Olympic Games, Peter Robeson, reserve rider in 1952, Major Ronnie Dallas, and Capt. the Hon. John Brooke. The girls included in the training were Mrs. Bryan Marshall, who had made her name in the jumping world as Mary Whitehead, her cousin Susan Whitehead, Dawn Pale-thorpe, and myself.

The horses were to be chosen from Aherlow and Nize-fela, who were both ridden at Helsinki, and Craven A who had been the reserve, The Monarch, Marmion, November's Eve, Nobbler, Scorchin', Earlsrath Rambler, and Flanagan.

Major Gibbon, Lt. Col. Talbot-Ponsonby, and some of the ten riders who wanted to keep out the biting March winds that swept coldly over the Ascot heath, set to with spades and dug ditches and water jumps ready for the horses to train over. The spare earth from the excava-tions was carefully turfed into little banks. When the fences were ready we found the letters G.G. R.I.P. neatly studded in pebbles on one formidable and grave-like bank. No one was quite sure if this was a warning to horses likely to make a fatal mistake at this fence, or

[216]

whether it referred to our team manager, with his initials, who had worked so hard in making these terrifying bunkers.

One of the main objects of the training, was to get the horses jumping wide doubles and trebles easily and with confidence. All our horses could jump the ordinary upright fences when ridden accurately, but in England they had not all met the doubles of spread fences with a long stride between them. Once the horses realized that they had to lengthen their stride as they landed, these difficult combinations caused no trouble.

As the training progressed, various horses fell by the wayside. Two went lame, and the riders were reduced in numbers like the ten little nigger boys. Duggie Stewart and John Brooke soon had no horses, and then Sue Whitehead broke her collar bone.

By the time we had ridden in public trials at Beaconsfield, Taunton, Badminton and Woolwich, jumping full rounds over Olympic-type fences, the team had more or less consolidated. Wilf White was going in great form on Nizefela with Nobbler as second horse, because Nobbler's owner, Mrs. Marshall, had to spend part of her time looking after her two baby boys. Peter Robeson was riding Craven A and also tried with Aherlow and Marmion. Dawn Palethorpe was riding Earlsrath Rambler and I had Flanagan and Scorchin'.

This was eventually the team that left for Lucerne, our only international show before the closing of entries for the Olympic Games. The sole difference was that Ronnie Dallas came as an individual with Marmion, and I took Prince Hal.

We arrived at Lucerne in glorious sunny weather and

four horses and riders were allowed to compete from each nation. The result was that Flanagan won the jump-off by five seconds from an Italian lady, so the gentlemen had to be content with third place and downwards!

Another interesting point was that although my horses had given me enough points to be leading rider throughout the show, the committee had divided this prize into two—the leading gentleman rider and the leading lady rider, so I had to be content with only the second title!

Lt. Col. Mike Ansell, together with Harry Llewellyn, arrived in time to give us support for the main event of the show. In the Nations Cup, our form had made our team the favourites. We paraded in glorious sunshine before the event with each national anthem being played as the team were presented to the President of Switzerland. As the notes of the last anthem faintly echoed across the lake, the sky darkened and a jagged glare of lightning rent the clouds. The clap of thunder that followed scattered the horses, and we quickly left the arena as the torrential rain and hail cascaded down. The ground became a lake, and then after an hour the rain stopped and the course was well cindered before we started jumping. In spite of the bad luck with the weather, the committee, who did so much for the competitors, always managed to overcome all handicaps by their efficient and cheerful organization.

Our team did not suffer from the water-logged ground, although Nizefela had a fall at the water jump after easily clearing all the other fences. Luckily neither he nor Wilf White were hurt, but we all held our breath until they both safely scrambled up out of the mud. Our other horses Flanagan, Earlsrath Rambler and Scorchin' were all clear in both rounds except for five faults notched up by the latter in his first round.

The next best team were the Swiss who finished with sixteen faults in front of the Argentine team who were third with twenty faults.

The training during the spring had thus proved its value at this point, and all our horses returned home fit and well before the final phase and the journey to Stockholm.

CHAPTER X

Olympic Games 1956

STOCKHOLM suddenly became a reality. At one moment we were jumping our final training round at Swindon and it seemed to be only the next moment when we were in the aeroplane taking us to Scandinavia.

We arrived late at night after flying north from Copenhagen over the many lakes and pine forests that pattern the Swedish countryside. As we came into the airport buildings to go through the customs and passport controls, we were attacked by the most vicious mosquitoes thirsting for delicious English blood of Olympic quality. These mosquitoes were a plague to ourselves and our horses throughout our stay and we were told that work had to be stopped in the forests during the summer, especially in Lapland, entirely through the mosquitoes.

We were driven into the town through the dense traffic and over the central island of the old city, with its pleasant coloured sandstone buildings. People were standing on the great ramps that lead up one side of the Royal Palace, while others crowded our road that led along by the harbour. Many were admiring the elegant lines of the Royal Yacht *Britannia*, which had arrived earlier that day bringing our Queen and Prince Philip on their State Visit to Stockholm. Another attractive feature of the harbour was a three-masted training yacht permanently moored there. Then there were the fishing boats with their bell-shaped nets suspended overhead, and as a contrast the *Britannia's* escort ships dominated the rest of the harbour.

I was relieved when the horses arrived safely by plane the following day, together with Paul who was looking after Flanagan. The six horses that had flown over, Nizefela, Flanagan, Scorchin', Earlsrath Rambler, Craven A and Nobbler, were all installed at the military school, where there was a wonderful covered riding school. It was the biggest indoor manège I have ever seen, and some of the dressage horses were being worked there when we arrived. Nearly all the horses from the twenty-nine nations represented in the Equestrian Games were stabled in the same yard and, from early in the morning until night-time, there was continued activity with horses coming and going for exercise and training.

On Sunday, June 10th, we paraded in the Opening Ceremony of the Equestrian events of the 1956 Olympiad. The Stadium in Stockholm was built especially for the 1912 Olympic Games and there was plenty of sandy ground nearby where we could work over jumps. In the morning after exercising our horses to ensure that they would behave after their easy journey the day before, we changed for the parade. Just before 2 p.m. the sky darkened, obliterating the hot sunshine of the morning and previous day, and a terrible thunderstorm broke over the district. Luckily, the rain had about stopped by the time we had to assemble and form up in alphabetical order of nations behind our respective flags.

We waited in the woods by the stadium for a long time, with the horses fidgeting from the plague of mosquitoes. Maybe it was during this long wait that Flanagan caught a slight chill on his loins.

In the meantime the King and Queen of Sweden and our Queen and Prince Philip arrived in open carriages. As they entered the stadium, the sun shone through the thunder clouds to greet them as a good omen for the Games.

The ceremony started with the entrance of the Royal Guard. The thirty riders were dressed in magnificent blue uniforms with white helmets, all mounted on quality chestnut horses to complete the impressive picture. Sweden with their Royal Guard and ourselves with the Household Cavalry must be the only countries left with such inspiring royal mounted escorts. The playing of the military bands was followed by the parade of the twenty-nine competing nations. By the time we came into the arena the grass was already full of neatly arranged teams. We were near the end of the line, our nation being Stor-Britannien in Swedish rather than being near the beginning of the alphabet as Great Britain. As we entered, our horses were initiated into the tremendous noise from the crowded stands. Our three show jumpers were fairly accustomed to appplause and so behaved reasonably well but the excitement was too much for our three-day event horses, who, in spite of their concentrated degree of dressage training, behaved abominably. Countryman in particular did not show any respect as we passed the Royal Box with his part-owner, our Queen watching his antics! He was not the only one to misbehave, as previously one of the first teams to come in had had a worse mishap, with William Steinkraus's horse of the U.S.A. jumping team rearing up and slipping over on its back just in front of the Royal Box!

When all the teams were lined across the grass behind their respective flags, the Olympic flag was brought in by six riders and hoisted at the end of the arena. The cannons were fired and the pigeons released from the top of the stadium entrance to circle round in a cloud and then fly away with a whirl of wings, taking the news of the Opening to their respective countries.

Prince Bertil came down from the Royal Box to read the Olympic oath in beautifully spoken Swedish, English, French and German. The Olympic hymn was sung by the choir after an introduction of bugles.

The Games having been declared open, a rider then entered the arena with the Olympic torch. The flame had been flown to Malmo and from there, in the south of Sweden, a relay of riders had brought it to Stockholm. The last rider cantered elegantly around the cinders of the arena track, holding the flaming torch aloft. He then lit the Olympic fire in the bowl at the entrance of the arena. Two runners, a girl and a man, lit torches from the rider's flame and ran with them down each side of the arena to the towers at the far corners. The flames were lit on the tops of the towers and a murmur of approval came from the crowd. We had also heard a murmur of approval from the Spanish team standing next to us, as the lovely girl in her white tights ran with floating strides across the arena. She was as pretty as she was good at Gymnastics, for which she had won the Gold Medal in the 1952 Games. The man was Eriksson, another Swedish gold medallist, winner of the 1500 metres in 1948 at Wembley.

The Bishop of Stockholm blessed the Games before we filed out of the arena. The Royal families left after seeing a display of folk dancing, gay with the colours of the Swedish national costumes.

We worked our horses early each morning before flies could pester them too much. On the Tuesday, two days after the Parade and only five days before our Olympic event, we jumped a few fences for the British T.V. newsreel. Flanagan was not at all happy and his quarters kept collapsing, so, needless to say, he hit three fences, an almost unknown occurrence for him. The next day he was not much better, as a kidney complaint does not clear up in twelve hours. However, from then on he gradually got better and was fit by Sunday.

The Three-Day event team had already done extremely well in the dressage part of their competition. On the second day of this event, the Wednesday, we went to see them jumping the cross-country course. We had already been up at 5 a.m. to work our horses, before the start of the endurance test at 8 a.m. I felt very depressed about Flanagan's trouble, and our trainer was worried because the team would have to be reshuffled if Flanagan was not fit to jump by the time the horses were declared on Saturday.

It started to pour with rain when we got to the cross-country course, and so our difficulties were partly forgotten while watching the competitors coping with the huge and solid fences, with the added hazard of very slippery ground on the take-off at some of the fences. The loose, wet earth on the bank of the trakener, twenty-second of the course of thirty-three jumps, caused much of the trouble which involved twenty of the fifty horses in getting penalty points. It was this fence that gave Countryman his fall, with his hindlegs skidding down the bank and into the deep ditch, as he tried to take off and jump over the post and rails built in the ditch and across to the other bank. Due to the calmness and presence of mind of his rider, Bertie Hill, the horse was extricated in a few seconds, after it had been submerged in the ditch, and then rejumped the whole fence with a magnificent leap from the top of one bank to the far side. It shows the courage of a horse like Countryman to take on a fence with such liberty, after an awful fall and the shock of slipping, through no fault of his own.

There was one diversion during the morning's jumping. Although competitors were started on the cross country phase at five-minute intervals, a Swiss had got into trouble and the next competitor, a German, had caught up with him. The German gave the tired Swiss horse a lead over the fence where he had refused, and from there on the two horses, enjoying each other's company, jumped the course together. Occasionally the Swiss would have a lead of a length or so and then the German would be in front. At the last fence, a solid parapet with a drop on the landing side, the German had a cracking fall and lost his horse. However, the Swiss, showing his Olympic spirit, galloped after the loose horse and brought it back, so that the German could finish his ride and save his team from elimination.

All our team finished safely with only penalties for one refusal from Kilbarry and Wild Venture. They both stopped at the seventh fence, a high post-and-rails in a ditch. Most of the horses seemed to come through the day's endurance test far better than many of the spectators, who were definitely not fit for a boggy morning's walk. In fact, the next day all the horses that had finished the course passed the vet, and yet some of their two-legged supporters from the cross country, were far from sound.

The team and individual placing was unaltered at the end of the jumping, giving us the thrill of seeing our team get their Gold Medals. The excitement of the crowd was great as a Swede, Petrus Kastenman, received his individual Gold Medal, and Frank Weldon had his well-deserved invidual bronze medal. Great credit was also given to the Commonwealth teams, with the Canadians, who had been training at Badminton, and the Australians, who had been at Aldershot for nearly a year, coming third and fourth to beat many more experienced horses and riders.

During the beginning of this week, I had spent part of one day seeing some of the islands of the Archipelago. Mr. Torsten Kreuger most kindly took me on his yacht, which he had designed and built from aluminium. She had every possible comfort and her maximum speed of twenty-six knots took us out to the Baltic in the minimum of time. To find a way through the maze of thousands of islands in the approaches to Stockholm must need most careful navigation and knowledge of the channels. I was told how the radar apparatus had helped this yacht to find the *Britannia* when she was waiting in the fog outside the Archipelago. All the journalists crowded in as well to see what had happened.

After groping their way to the Royal yacht hidden in the fog, the return journey was well marked by the trail of floating beer bottles, thrown overboard on the way out by the thirsty journalists!

We landed on some of the islands and, in spite of drenching rain and fog that spoilt our view, I saw a sea eagle's nest. The pile of loose sticks filled the whole top of the pine tree, which needed the full strength of the trunk to support the house of this monstrous and very rare bird.

The next day our team had the honour of an invitation to a cocktail party given by Her Majesty the Queen aboard the *Britannia*. During this wonderful party, where I overheard one appreciative remark that Her Majesty certainly knew how to mix a dry Martini, we learned that the Riding School, next to where our horses were stabled, had caught fire. I had only just left the stables shortly before, where the vet had been looking at Flanagan, so I was sure that Paul would still be with the horses. Luckily, none of the stables caught fire, although it was a tragedy to see the lovely Riding School completely gutted the next day. The fire must have been caused by a careless person throwing a cigarette-end into some bales of straw stored against the outer wall. Directly the bale burst into flame, a spark caught the inflammable roof, which was burning fiercely from end to end within minutes, with flames leaping fifty feet into the air. Our horses were the nearest to the fire, but they were able to return to their boxes after waiting outside until the roof of the manège collapsed and there was no more danger from sparks.

Later that evening I was able to drown the Flanagan

worries with music, listening to an excellent concert that included Brahms' First Symphony. We were also invited to have some vodka with the Russian team, who were staying in the Karlberg barracks which had been converted into one of the two camps for Olympic teams. The riders in the jumping team could only speak Russian, but their *chef de mission*, General Ebel, could speak some French. So through his interpreting, I was able to talk to their girl rider, who was the only other lady rider entered in the Olympic Grand Prix jumping competition. Her name was Tatiana Koulikovskaia, and she was interested to find out about the organization and training schedule for our jumpers. All their team lived in Moscow, and she had not jumped abroad before. Their horses were state-owned and kept in a centre near Moscow, with excellent jumping paddocks and indoor schools. There were many shows during the year for the horses to gain competitive experience, but they often had to travel great distances. It was for this reason and the expense involved, that the Russian team had not been seen outside their country except for the Olympic Games in Helsinki and now at Stockholm. Although the Russian public enjoyed seeing jumping events and there were always crowds of spectators at their shows, the competitors could not win money prizes, but just some token of honour, such as a cup.

Tatiana and the best of their riders called Vladimir Raspopov wanted to know the exact training of our horses at home. I told them that it depended on the weather and how I felt, and also on how the horse felt. The Russians were amused that I did not keep to a strict plan of perhaps Monday, two hours' walking exercise;

Tuesday, one hour's schooling on the flat; Wednesday, jump eight fences, etc.

Unfortunately we did not see Tatiana jump, as she had had a fall earlier in the week and was suffering from slight delayed concussion. However, Brigitte Schockaert was substituted into the Belgian team, to make one other lady competitor. Her horse Muscadin finished with 59 faults.

We were back at the Karlberg barracks at 6 a.m. on Sunday the 17th, each with a plan of the course to look at during breakfast. Just before 7 a.m. most of the riders were gathered at the entrance of the arena, waiting for the clock to strike so that they could walk the course and examine the fences. We knew the fences were going to be big and our fears were justified when we saw that they were up to all expectations in size and width. As well as this, they were placed closely together, which allowed little time for recovery once a mistake had been made.

I met a Spaniard who said that although he had gone to bed early, for nearly the first time in his life, he had not been able to sleep a wink except for a moment when he had dreamed of jumps as big as cathedrals, and here was his nightmare come true. Other worried-looking riders who had small or not very brave horses, were stepping out the wide distances between the combinations of fences.

The make-up of the spreads ensured that the horses could only put one stride, where normally two would be taken. The worst problem was set at fence No. 5 a double of silver birch fences. This followed closely upon a rounded wooden wall with a 5 foot 3 inch pole

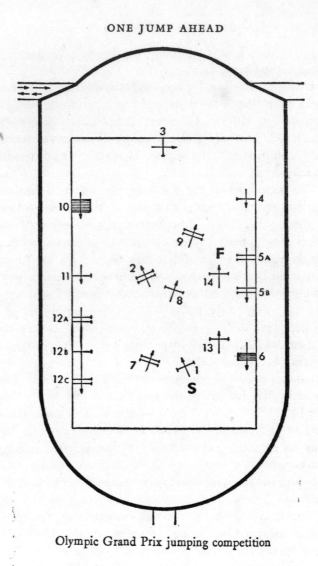

Olympic Grand Prix jumping competition

No.	Type of Obstacle	Height	Width
1	Sloping hedge with pole	4′ 5″	3′ 8½″
2	Swedish fence	4′ 3″–4′ 5″	5′ 7″
3	Manor gate from Stäringe	4′ 11½″	—
4	South African pigsty	5′ 3″	4′ 11″
5A	Birch poles	4′ 5″–4′ 7″	4′ 11″
5B	Birch-gates with poles	4′ 7″–4′ 9″	5′ 7″
6	Water jump with stationata	4′ 11″	7′ 0½″
7	Low wall with double parallel bars	4′ 11″–5′ 3″	6′ 6½″
8	Paling	5′ 3″	—
9	Bank with water-ditch and poles	4′ 9″–5′ 1¼″	7′ 2½″
10	Water jump	—	16′ 4½″
11	Irish garden wall	4′ 11¾″	1′ 7½″
12A	Oxer	4′ 7½″–4′ 9″	5′ 3″
12B	Fun fair gates with pole	5′ 1″	—
12C	Open oxer	4′ 7″–4′ 9″	5′ 7″
13	Garden fence from the Riviera	5′ 3″	—
14	Park wall	5′ 3″	2′ 7½″

Order of fences, 1–14; Length of course, 775 m.; Speed, 400 m/min.
Time allowed, 108.8 seconds; Time limit, 217.6 seconds.

Flanagan was in fine form and sailed over the first fence and carefully jumped the following parallel bars, a rather flimsy and unimpressive fence. We turned across the arena to the rounded gate, which we jumped in the corner where it was at least 8 inches lower than in the centre. Now we had the first of the lines to tackle. The great brown wooden wall Flanagan cleared by a foot. Coming down from this height into the mud slowed him up considerably, and in five strides we had not been able to build up enough impetus for the double. He jumped in all right, but with his short stride he could not clear the spread of the out. He reached hard, with all the freedom that I could give him, and caught the far pole just behind his elbows. How he did not fall I cannot imagine, but he took the pole with him for a stride or two, leaving the rest of the fence fit only for Swedish match-sticks, and without a tremor leapt the open ditch and 5 foot poles with complete confidence. Everything went well then until the treble fence No. 12, where, in the effort to get the spreads of the first and last part, he just toppled off the pole of the middle jump. The last two straight fences gave him no trouble, to finish with a total of eight faults.

It was not until Winkler, the third of the German team, went on Halla that our faults were bettered. Halla, fresh from her recent triumphs in Germany, was jumping a lovely smooth round, although she bounced the poles of the treble without displacing them. Then at fence No. 13, a straight barrier made of bamboo grass, which we had been sorely tempted to put a match to during our inspection of the course in the morning, Winkler nearly met his Waterloo. He was a

little close for the take-off and Halla made a great effort.
Winkler, gripping suddenly, wrenched a muscle in his
groin and very nearly fell off as he landed. He was
rolling in the saddle as he approached the last fence,
where he got four faults as he pulled the mare
through, just managing to finish but obviously in
great pain.

Voulette, with Jonquères d'Oriola, the individual
Gold Medallist of the Games at Helsinki, then jumped
best of any small horse during the day, having seven
faults in her first and eight in her second round. Wilf
White came near the end with Nizefela, to jump an
excellent round for eight faults, having down the last
parallel bars of the triple fence and then the last straight
fence.

Before the start of the second round at 4 p.m. our
team was standing second with thirty-two faults to the
Germans' twenty-eight faults and the Italians' thirty-
nine faults.

The sun had come out and the ground had improved
considerably by the time our Queen arrived to see the
second stage of the battle. The first German horse,
Ala, halved his first score to eight faults, and then
Uruguay came in to do the best round so far with only
three faults, for a stop at the third fence, the gate.
Scorchin' increased our score with five fences down,
and then the second round began with Thiedemann.
He made one mistake, bringing his total to twelve faults
for the two rounds. Oppes on Pagoro did not fare so
well for Italy, collecting twenty-four faults, one more
than his previous round.

I was the next combatant in this battle between three

nations. We only needed a clear round! Flanagan could not have been more co-operative. He stretched himself to his utmost and cleared the awful double; he tried as hard as he could when clearing the big spread fence No. 7—more parallel bars. We started the line from the water jump away from the entrance of the arena, and he checked slightly as he landed over the water. We met the wall on a short stride and he was unable to lengthen his stride quickly enough to get the pace necessary for the treble. He hit the first parallels, pitched on landing and could not possibly jump the next and so stopped. We galloped back to the wall and turned, so that the clock would stop while the fence was being repaired.

When we got going again, we jumped in with full pace, but still Flanagan could not quite reach the last parallel bars and just toppled off the farthest pole. So, with thirteen faults gleaned from this one combination, he finished clear over the last two fences.

I had the rest of the competition to think over how else I could have ridden that line of fences. Perhaps if I had used my whip from before the water until after the last parallel bars he might have forced more impulsion. On the other hand, his balance might have been upset or he would have had to lengthen too much, jumping flat and not high enough. Anyway, I could have murdered myself for not riding that line differently, for Flanagan had been giving his very best while jumping these fences that were at the limit of his scope.

The next stir of excitement came when Winkler entered the ring on Halla. He had been given some morphia to ease the pain from his muscle and he obviously had no grip. The crowd held their breath and in the silence of the arena he began his round. The mare pricked her ears and jumped the smoothest clear round possible, with her rider unable to sit forward in his usual balance and shouting with pain as she jumped each fence. He earned a tremendous ovation as he finished with a total of only four faults to ensure his individual Gold Medal.

Raimundo d'Inzeo followed him into the ring with Merano, who emulated Halla's performance, giving the crowd their only other clear round of the day and the second in sequence. This faultless round made the Italians only one point behind us, and we still had one rider to go. Wilf White and Nizefela went brilliantly again, but, alas, just had the parallel bars of the seventh fence. So the final team placings were: Germany the Gold Medals with a total of forty faults, Italy the silver medals with sixty-six penalties, and ourselves the bronze, with sixty-nine. Fourth were the Argentina team with a total of ninety-nine and a half faults.

Altogether ten teams finished in the order: U.S.A. (who were fifth), Spain, Ireland, France, Switzerland and Brazil, who made two hundred and twenty-eight and a half faults. The team results were a considerable improvement on the 1948 Games, when only three teams finished the course. The whole standard of jumping has improved since then and, although this was a bigger course than jumped at the previous post-war Games, the teams who had not been in regular international competitions suffered the consequences. One Egyptian rider, who was preparing his horse while I was working on Flanagan, came sadly up to me. He said, 'I hear on the loud-speaker that my team mate has eighty-eight and a half faults. How can it be? I work it out. With every one of the seventeen fences down, that only makes sixty-eight faults. Two refusals, all he is allowed, is another nine, then we only get seventy-seven faults!' I left him shaking his head, and wondered if he would remember that a fall costs eight faults and also there was a possibility of time penalties!

After the competition the individual winners received their medals, with Winkler, followed by the brothers Raimundo and Piero d'Inzeo. Then the three teams came in for their presentation, and after saluting the Olympic flag we made a tour of honour, again saluting the Royal Box as we passed.

We left the arena and the jumps were quickly cleared for the closing ceremony and the extinguishing of the Olympic fire. That night, after seeing to the horses and changing, we did not arrive at the official party until about midnight. I certainly did not get to bed very early by the time we had dined and danced and said our good-byes to the teams who were leaving directly. Imagine my pleasure when I was woken at 8 a.m. by the telephone. A journalist in London wished to know why I had hit the twelfth fence the day before. I told him that I had not jumped high enough, and went to sleep again.

That day, in the same arena, we jumped in the first competition of the C.H.I.O. (Concours Hippique International Officiel). The evening was grey and cold and there were about one hundred horses to jump in the competition, although the Olympic horses were not allowed to take part. When we walked round the normal course, the jumps looked microscopic after the giants of the day before. It all seemed an anticlimax.

The next day Flanagan beat many of his Olympic opponents over a course more within his scope when he won the 'Hederspris'. Prince Hal followed this up by being third in the Puissance. The ground, which had dried up very quickly since the rain on Sunday, was too hard for him, and he was afraid of landing from great heights and jarring himself, so Thiedemann on Meteor and Peter Robeson on Scorchin' fought out the finish with Meteor winning on the final barrage.

In the Nations Cup the next day, it was thought that our team and the Italians would have to fight it out, as the Germans had lost Winkler, who was hobbling about on a stick after his injury. This proved to be the closest fight that I have ever known in a Nations Cup. We finished our two rounds with exactly the same faults and had to have a jump off. Some of the fences were raised, and as it was late the floodlights were switched on. However, if there had been time to wait for an hour or so it would again have been light, as there is practically no night in Sweden at midsummer.

The first horse in was Uruguay, who had four faults at a narrow two strides double. Piero had tried to make his horse jump it with one stride, but after the Olympic effort and two more days' jumping, Uruguay did not co-operate. Dawn Palethorpe then jumped an excellent round on Earlsrath Rambler. Oppes, the next Italian to go, had an unlucky fall, causing an abundance of faults. We were clear again with Peter Robeson on Scorchin'. Although Raimundo d'Inzeo had no faults on Merano, Flanagan was also clear, meaning that we had no faults for our team, before our fourth member, Wilf White, had jumped. The Italians could not do better than four faults even if their last horse was clear, so, before the last round, we had won the Nations Cup.

After the last competition at the end of the show, Flanagan came into the arena for the presentation of my prize for the best lady rider throughout the show. We made our tour of honour and thus Flanagan was the last of the jumpers to leave the equestrian battleground of the sixteenth Olympiad.